T0080730

PRESENTED TO:

....

FROM:

....

DATE:

....

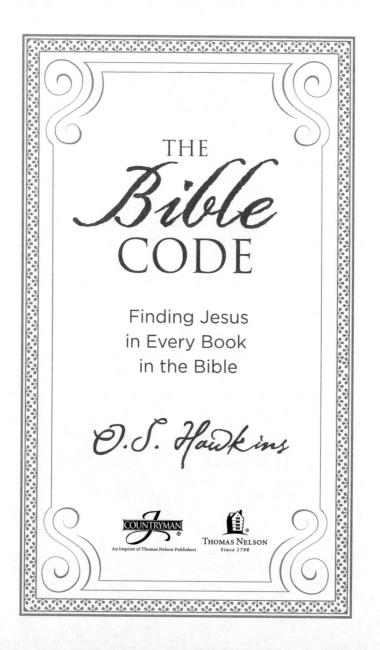

THE
Bible
CODE

Finding Jesus
in Every Book
in the Bible

O. S. Hawkins

COUNTRYMAN®
An Imprint of Thomas Nelson Publishers

THOMAS NELSON
Since 1798

Published in Nashville, Tennessee, by Thomas Nelson. Thomas Nelson is a registered trademark of HarperCollins Christian Publishing, Inc.

Thomas Nelson titles may be purchased in bulk for educational, business, fund-raising, or sales promotional use. For information, please email SpecialMarkets@ThomasNelson.com.

ISBN: 978-1-4002-1780-9
ISBN: 978-1-4002-1785-4 (eBook)
ISBN: 978-1-4002-1819-6 (audiobook)

Printed in China

21 22 23 24 25 26 SKY 10 9 8 7 6 5 4

CONTENTS

INTRODUCTION

*T*he cross is the hinge upon which the door of all human history turns. Its immediate impact on Jesus' followers was total despair, defeat, even doubt. The Scriptures pointedly proclaim that "all the disciples forsook Him and fled" (Matthew 26:56). Two of those dejected disciples on the way home to Emmaus lamented, "We had hoped that he was the one" (Luke 24:21 ESV). But they left that hope buried in the tomb of Joseph of Arimathea outside the city walls of Jerusalem. While they were in the depths of discouragement, those words had just escaped their lips when they noticed someone walking alongside them on the road. It was the Lord! He was alive. "And beginning at Moses and all the Prophets, He expounded to them in all the Scriptures the things concerning Himself" (v. 27).

Yes, Jesus declared from the very beginning of the Bible with the first five books of Moses and continuing "in all the Scriptures" that He was there on every page. He was that ram on Abraham's altar in Genesis. He was the Passover lamb in Exodus. He was the cloud by day and the pillar of fire by night that led the Israelites in the book of Numbers. He was the fourth man in the midst of the burning fiery furnace in the book of Daniel. He was there in every book of the Bible, sometimes in type, sometimes in shadow, sometimes in prophecy. Jesus—this scarlet thread of redemption—can be found woven through every book in sacred Scripture. Near the beginning of His public ministry, Jesus challenged His followers to "search the Scriptures, for in them you think you have eternal life; and these are they which testify of Me" (John 5:39). He continued, "If you believed Moses, you would believe Me; for he wrote about Me" (v. 46).

> Jesus can be found woven through every book in sacred Scripture.

Perhaps you have never thought about the fact that Jesus can be found in every book of the Bible. He is not simply to be found in the four Gospels of the New Testament. He is there from Genesis 1:1 to Revelation 22:21. The Bible is the Jesus Book. The Old Testament conceals Him in type and shadow. The New Testament reveals Him in all His manifest glory. The Bible is like a flower. The Old Testament is the bud. The New Testament is the bloom.

The Old Testament is a book of shadows depicting progressive images of our coming Redeemer. The apostle Paul spoke of this as being "a shadow of things to come" (Colossians 2:17). There must be two elements in producing a shadow.

To produce a shadow there needs to be a light and an image. Behind the words of Scripture is a great Light shining on the image of Christ casting His shadow across its pages. The clarity of any shadow depends on the angle with which the light strikes the body. I can stand in the sunlight in the early morning hours when it is rising and my shadow is completely out of proportion. It stretches all the way across the street and onto the building behind me. However, as the sun continues to rise, the shorter and more revealing my shadow becomes. At midmorning, when it is at a forty-five-degree angle, my shadow is the perfect shape of my body. As I continue to stand in place and when the sun reaches its zenith at high noon, the shadow disappears and only my body is seen.

And so it is with the revelation of Christ in the Bible. When the sun of revelation begins to shine way back in the early chapters of Genesis, the shadow is dim and a bit faint. As the chapters unfold and more light appears, Christ comes into sharper focus. By the time we reach Isaiah, chapter 53, there appears the perfect shadow of the One who would be "smitten by God, and afflicted. . . . wounded for our transgressions, . . . bruised for our iniquities; . . . [and] led as a lamb to the slaughter" (vv. 4–7). When we turn the page from Malachi 4:6 to Matthew 1:1, it is high noon on God's clock, the shadows disappear, and we see Jesus! No more shadows of Him. No more types. No more prophecies. Just Jesus.

The Bible Code is designed to take us on a journey to find Jesus in every book of the Bible. And, in finding Him, we find life . . . not just eternal in the then and there, but abundant in the here and now. And the bottom line? All the Bible, and all of life for that matter, is about Jesus, the very "author and finisher of our faith" (Hebrews 12:2). Let's turn the page and begin the great adventure of finding Jesus in Genesis, the first book of the Bible.

1 FINDING JESUS IN GENESIS

He Is the Ram at Abraham's Altar

Then [God] said, "Take now your son, your only son Isaac, whom you love, and go to the land of Moriah, and offer him there as a burnt offering on one of the mountains of which I shall tell you." . . . And [the Angel of the LORD] said, "Do not lay your hand on the lad, or do anything to him; for now I know that you fear God, since you have not withheld your son, your only son, from Me."

Then Abraham lifted his eyes and looked, and there behind him was a ram caught in a thicket by its horns. So Abraham went and took the ram, and offered it up for a burnt offering instead of his son.
—GENESIS 22:2, 12–13

*A*nyone who has ever seen a picture of the Holy City of Jerusalem has most likely seen the golden-domed Mosque of Omar, more commonly referred to as the Dome of the Rock, sitting center stage and glistening in the bright Middle Eastern sun on the summit of Mount Moriah. It was on, or very near, the same spot where Solomon's temple, in all its magnificent glory, once sat. The temple's massive foundation stones, quarried from the northern side of the mountain, shaped and then moved to the summit, are an architectural marvel to this very day. The temple's construction materials consisted of 2,000 tons of gold and 7,500 pounds of silver. There, the Jews from around the world would make their pilgrimage for the annual sacrifice during their High Holy Days.

But centuries before a Muslim mosque or a Jewish temple sat on that site, one lone man, accompanied by his only son, scaled the summit of that same mountain and constructed a simple altar of sacrifice. God had promised Abraham that he was the one chosen to be the father of a great nation—a nation whose descendants would be as numerous as the stars of the heavens. But there was a bit of a problem. He was already an old man, and his wife, Sarah, was decades beyond childbearing years. As though that were not problematic enough, she was also barren, having been unable to produce a child over the course of her entire life. Then came a miracle birth, not a virgin birth, but a miracle all the same. Isaac, through whom the world would be blessed by the eventual appearance of the Messiah, was born to Abraham and Sarah.

Times of blessing in life are often followed by times of testing. And so it was for Abraham. Isaac, this only son of Abraham and Sarah, was the heir who would carry forward God's promise to Abraham. But God now instructed the father to sacrifice his son as a test of his trust. God wanted to know that Abraham's faith was in His promise, not in his son, Isaac.

> Times of blessing in life are often followed by times of testing.

Times have not changed much across the centuries. Many of us who have been so richly blessed by God can be tempted to transfer our trust from the One who blesses us to the blessings we have and hold.

Abraham's response to this seemingly impossible challenge was one of faith, obedience, and trust in his God. There was no doubt, no defiance, no delay. He simply took God at His word, and the New Testament writer of Hebrews framed it thus: "By faith Abraham obeyed. . . . Therefore from one man, and him as good as dead, were born as many as the stars of the sky in multitude—innumerable as the sand which is by the seashore. . . . By faith Abraham, when he was tested, offered up Isaac, and he who had received the promises offered up his only begotten son" (Hebrews 11:8, 12, 17).

This trek of father and son up Mount Moriah is replete with one picture after another of a journey that would be taken some two thousand years later to the same mountain by our own heavenly Father accompanied by His only begotten Son and our Savior, the Lord Jesus Christ. Upon arriving at the foot of the mount of sacrifice, Abraham instructed his servant to stay there, saying, "The lad and I will go yonder and worship, and we will come back to you" (Genesis 22:5). What was about to take place on that summit was a transaction between father and son alone. The same would be true at

Mount Calvary (the northern extension of Mount Moriah). During those three hours of darkness while Jesus was on the cross, God the Father and God the Son did business alone. The agony of those hours was indescribable. While the final sacrifice for the sins of the world was being made, God closed the door to all human eyes and turned out the lights of heaven. For three hours, the eternal transaction for your sin and mine was between the Father and the Son alone.

Look closely at Abraham. He "took the wood of the burnt offering and laid it on Isaac his son" (v. 6) as they journeyed up the mountain. This is a portent, a foreshadow, of the divine side of Calvary. Much of our thoughts concerning the cross are from the human side, what it means for us. But think of the divine side. Look at the Father's heart as He placed the wooden cross upon the bruised and bloodied back of His own Son and watched as He carried it up the way to Golgotha, the place of execution.

As they journeyed along together, Isaac, bearing the wood for the sacrifice upon his back, made an inquiry of his father: "Where is the lamb for a burnt offering?" (v. 7). Quick came Abraham's response: "'My son, God will provide for Himself the lamb.' . . . So the two of them went together" (v. 8). Yes! God Himself will provide the lamb. In fact, God Himself *will be* the Lamb, the sacrifice for our sin. It was of this very event and to these very words that Jesus addressed the Jews, saying, "Your father Abraham rejoiced to see My day, and he saw it and was glad" (John 8:56).

Arriving at the summit of Moriah, Abraham meticulously built an altar; arranged the wood for the burnt offering upon it; then bound his son, Isaac; and laid him upon the altar. Then he "stretched out his hand and took the knife to slay his son" (Genesis 22:10). Immediately, the Angel of the Lord (the preincarnate Christ Himself) called to him from heaven, "'Do not lay your hand on the lad . . . for now I know that you fear God, since you have not withheld your son, your only son, from Me.' Then Abraham lifted his eyes and looked, and there behind him was a ram caught in a thicket by its horns. So Abraham went and took the ram, and offered it up . . . instead of his son" (vv. 12–14).

> The Angel of the Lord . . . called to him from heaven, "Do not lay your hand on the lad."

Our imaginations can only wonder what must have been racing through Abraham's mind that day. Fifty years before, God had promised him a son. Thirty years passed, and God repeated the promise. It would take a miracle. But Abraham believed. Paul would later say, "Abraham believed God, and it was accounted to him for righteousness" (Romans 4:3). God kept His word. And Isaac was born and grew up. Then God tested Abraham, and when he kept the faith, God provided a substitutionary sacrifice, a ram. That ram is a beautiful picture of our Lord Jesus. You and I deserve to die, but Jesus provided Himself for the lamb. He rushed out to Calvary and took our place, bore our sin, died our death so we could live His life. He took our sin so we could take His righteousness. He is our substitutionary sacrifice and all-sufficient Savior!

"And Abraham called the name of the place, The-LORD-Will-Provide; as it is said to this day, 'In the Mount of the LORD it shall be provided'" (Genesis 22:14). If there is any doubt that Abraham understood what was happening that day, Jesus settled it two millennia later. When traversing those same dusty roads, He said, "Your father Abraham rejoiced to see My day, and he saw it and was glad" (John 8:56).

You and I have a God who can and will provide—who, in fact, provided Himself as our very own substitutionary sacrifice. No wonder when Jesus stepped from the obscurity of the carpenter's shop to appear in the Jordan Valley, John the Baptist thrust a pointed finger in His direction and shouted, "Behold! The Lamb of God who takes away the sin of the world!" (John 1:29). Yes, we can find Jesus in every book of the Bible, sometimes in type, sometimes in shadow, sometimes in prophecy. And here in Genesis? He is that ram at Abraham's altar, our own substitutionary sacrifice.

2 FINDING JESUS IN EXODUS

He Is Our Passover Lamb

"Every man shall take for himself a lamb . . . without blemish. . . . Kill it at twilight. . . . Take some of the blood and put it on the two doorposts and on the lintel of the houses. . . . Now the blood shall be a sign for you. . . . And when I see the blood, I will pass over you; and the plague shall not be on you to destroy you when I strike the land of Egypt."

—EXODUS 12:3, 5–7, 13

*F*or three and a half millennia one of the most important dates on the calendar for our Jewish friends is the evening each year when they celebrate the Passover Seder meal commemorating their deliverance from slavery in Egypt. For four centuries, they were slaves to Pharaoh and to Egypt. Then Moses returned from exile to be their emancipator, and God sent a series of plagues upon Egypt. The last was the most devastating: the death of all the firstborn throughout the entire land. To be spared the plague, the Jews were instructed to take a young lamb—perfect and without blemish—slay it, and spread its blood over the lintels and doorposts of their homes so that on the fateful night the Lord passed through, He would "see the blood" and "pass over." Every home where the blood was applied was spared the death of their firstborn. They were saved by the blood of the sacrificed lamb.

> They were saved by the blood of the sacrificed lamb.

That little lamb is a perfect picture of our coming Deliverer, the Lord Jesus Christ. Just as Christ was in the prime of life when He went to the cross, the lamb had to be a male of the first year. Just as Christ was perfect and without sin, the lamb was to be "without blemish." No wonder when Simon Peter spoke of Christ's sacrifice he declared that we are saved by "the precious blood of Christ, as of a lamb without blemish and without spot" (1 Peter 1:19). The description of this sacrificial Passover lamb is given in minute detail in Exodus, even to the specific instructions that not one of its bones was to be broken (Exodus 12:46). It is no wonder then that when the soldiers approached the cross, the Bible records, "But when they came to Jesus and saw that He was already dead, they did not break His legs. . . . These things were done that the Scripture should be fulfilled, 'Not one of His bones shall be broken'" (John 19:33, 36).

The Israelites were saved on that death-filled night because by faith they applied the blood of the lamb to the doorposts of their homes. What a poignant and prophetic picture for those of us living in this dispensation. The Bible says, "The soul who sins shall die" (Ezekiel 18:20). The only way we can be saved from judgment is by applying the blood of our sacrificial Lamb, the Lord Jesus Christ, to the doorposts of our heart by faith in Him alone.

Across the years my wife, Susie, and I have intentionally made friends with Jewish people from Los Angeles to Dallas to New York to Jerusalem. On many a Passover evening, we have sat with them at their Seder meals. The dining tables are always beautifully set with all the elements to remind them of their forefathers' deliverance from bondage. There is the shank bone of a lamb, the bitter herbs, the salt water, and all the other elements that give visual expression to their sojourn as they pass on their ancient tradition from generation to generation. For more than 3,500 years, the youngest family member seated at the table has asked the father four questions: Why is this night different from other nights, and on this night we eat only unleavened bread? Why on other nights do we eat all kinds of herbs, and on this night we eat only bitter herbs? Why on other nights do we not dip, but tonight we dip twice? Why on this night do we recline in our chairs at the table? The father then reads from the ancient Haggadah, the Passover book, explaining that the unleavened bread reminds them of the haste with which they had to leave Egypt, the bitter herbs of the bitterness of slavery and bondage, the dipping of parsley into the salt water of the deliverance through the Red Sea and the Egyptian army's drowning in their pursuit. And, finally, the reclining at the table expresses their freedom in no longer being slaves.

Fifteen hundred years following that first Passover, Jesus gathered His disciples in an upper room on Mount Zion in Jerusalem to commentate the Passover with those nearest and dearest to Him. He knew when He passed the bread and lifted the cup that in a few hours His own body would be broken for us and His own blood would be poured out to make a way to heaven for us. Applying the blood to the doorposts of those Israelite homes meant two things: freedom from slavery and deliverance from death. Applying the blood of Christ to our own lives means the same two things: freedom from slavery to sin, which has its way of binding us and enslaving us, and deliverance from spiritual death. It's no wonder Paul said, "The wages of sin is death, but the gift of God is eternal life in Christ Jesus our Lord" (Romans 6:23).

Our Lord must have had this Passover lamb in mind when He engaged the skeptical religious leaders after healing a man at the Pool of Bethesda. For He said, "Search the Scriptures, for in them you think you have eternal life; and these are they which testify of Me" (John 5:39). When we look hard enough, we find Jesus in every book of the Bible, and nowhere is He more perfectly presented than here in the book of Exodus. For it is here that we find Jesus, our very own Passover Lamb.

3 FINDING JESUS IN LEVITICUS

He Is Our Sweet-Smelling Aroma

"And the priest shall burn all on the altar as a burnt sacrifice, an offering made by fire, a sweet aroma to the LORD."

—LEVITICUS 1:9

*L*eviticus . . . it is one of those Old Testament books that we tend to quickly skim over when reading through the Bible. It can appear monotonous with its detailed minutia of all that was involved in the sacrificial system of burnt offerings in Jewish worship. Yet rising from these pages is the sweet-smelling aroma of Christ Himself. Leviticus provides us a most vivid foreshadowing of Christ's work of atonement and is the foundational offering in the Torah to understanding Christ's own sacrifice for us.

All the multiplied thousands of animal sacrifices in the Old Testament never took away a single sin. The writer of Hebrews is crystal clear about this: "For it is not possible that the blood of bulls and goats could take away sins" (10:4). They served to simply cover sins until Christ came, the perfect sacrifice, to take away all the sins of the world. We illustrate this truth every time we use a credit card to make a purchase. When our card is processed at the checkout counter, it is a promise to pay later when the bill from the credit card company arrives in our inbox or address. The card serves to cover the purchase until the final payment is made. Such were all the Old Testament sacrifices. They covered sins until the final payment to remove *all* sin would be paid on a hill called Golgotha, outside the city walls of Jerusalem.

From each of these sacrifices arose an aroma that was pleasing to God (Leviticus 1:9). The psalmist got a glimpse beyond these shadows when the preincarnate Christ spoke through him, saying, "Burnt offering and sin offering You did not require. Then I said, 'Behold, I come; in the scroll of the book it is written of me. I delight to do Your will, O my God, and Your law is within my heart'" (Psalm 40:6–8). Jesus came to do the Father's will, and that obedience took Him to His own place of execution where He became the final sacrifice for sin. For century upon century, the Jews traversed the known world and made their annual pilgrimages to Jerusalem to offer their sacrifices on the altar of the temple. The reason this ritual has vanished for the past two thousand years is no secret. There has not been a Jewish animal sacrifice on Mount Moriah in Jerusalem in all this time because, two thousand years ago, all the prophecies of those sacrifices were fulfilled in Christ when He became the final and complete sacrifice for the sins of the world. And, to tie the bow on it all, Paul said of Christ that He "loved us and

[gave] Himself for us, an offering and a sacrifice to God for a sweet-smelling aroma" (Ephesians 5:2).

But this sweet-smelling aroma does not end with Christ. Today, we who have placed our trust in Christ and know the forgiveness of sin are "the fragrance of Christ among those who are being saved . . . the aroma of life leading to life" (2 Corinthians 2:15–16). Think of it: you are a sweet-smelling aroma to God and a blessing to others.

Certain smells have a message all their own. Freshly cut grass, suntan oil, and hamburgers grilling outside speak of summer and its heat. The smells of cinnamon, evergreens, and baked cookies bring Christmas to mind. And

> You are a sweet-smelling aroma to God and a blessing to others.

the fragrance of Christ, transmitted by a believer in love with Him, lifts up a sweet-smelling aroma of worship that is well pleasing to God. Paul was alluding to this very truth when he wrote to the Philippians, saying, "Indeed I have all and abound. I am full, having received from Epaphroditus the things sent from you, a sweet-smelling aroma, an acceptable sacrifice, well pleasing to God" (Philippians 4:18). Yes, you are the fragrance of Christ.

This is our calling as believers, to give the world the fragrance of Christ when they are in our very presence. It was to this end that Paul admonished the Ephesians—and us—saying, "Therefore be imitators of God as dear children. And walk in love, as Christ also has loved us and given Himself for us, an offering and a sacrifice to God for a sweet-smelling aroma" (Ephesians 5:1–2). As we continue through the Bible on our journey of finding Jesus in every book, pause here for a moment in Leviticus and inhale a deep breath. The question is not, "Can you see it?" but, "Can you smell it? The sweet fragrance of Christ!"

"And the priest shall burn all on the altar as a burnt sacrifice, an offering made by fire, a sweet aroma to the LORD" (Leviticus 1:9). Jesus is in every book of the Bible.

4 FINDING JESUS IN NUMBERS

He Is the Bronze Serpent on Moses' Pole

Then the LORD said to Moses, "Make a fiery serpent, and set it on a pole; and it shall be that everyone who is bitten, when he looks at it, shall live." So Moses made a bronze serpent, and put it on a pole; and so it was, if a serpent had bitten anyone, when he looked at the bronze serpent, he lived.

—NUMBERS 21:8–9

*I*f we ever memorized a verse of Scripture, most likely it was John 3:16: "For God so loved the world that He gave His only begotten Son, that whoever believes in Him should not perish but have everlasting life." It is the one verse most often heard in the simplicity and beauty of a little child's voice proudly reciting their first verse from memory. This is the one verse that has been spoken by many older saints as they were breathing their final breaths and whispering these words through dying lips. It finds itself in Scripture, directly on the heels of Jesus' words, "As Moses lifted up the serpent in the wilderness, even so must the Son of Man be lifted up, that whoever believes in Him should not perish but have eternal life" (vv. 14–15).

One of the clues to understanding the Bible is to realize

that Jesus is in every book of the Bible. He may be there in shadow. He may be there in prophecy. Or He may be there—as in Numbers—in type. Numbers 21 presents one of the most beautiful types, or pictures, of our Lord on the cross found in the entire Bible. His own reference to this experience during the wilderness wandering adds credence to the message of the gospel.

The children of Israel, having emerged safely on the other side of the Red Sea, then faced a forty-year period of wandering in the wilderness. God led them with a cloud by day and a pillar of fire by night (Exodus 13:21). And by God's provision, they were fed each day with a bread-like substance called "manna" that sustained them and nourished them along the way (Exodus 16:4). But this was not enough for them. They began to gripe and complain to Moses. They didn't like the way they were being led, and they didn't like the way they were being fed.

God is holy, and the same Bible that says He is a God of love reveals He is also a God of justice who judges the rebellion of those He calls His own. "So the LORD sent fiery serpents among the people, and they bit the people; and many of the people of Israel died" (Numbers 21:6). These bites were "fiery" and painful. Their venom turned their victims' every nerve into a burning fever. And the bites were fatal. Many died on the spot. In panic and fear the people admitted their sin and called on Moses to ask God to take away the serpents.

God's remedy was to make a bronze serpent and put it on a pole, and then He promised that "everyone who is bitten, when he looks at it, shall live" (v. 8). God did not eradicate the serpents any more than He eradicates sin in our own lives. He did something much more incredible and sufficient—He put His own Son on a cross. Why a serpent of bronze? The serpent is a picture of sin in the Bible. When Christ hung on His cross, He took all the sin of the world in His own body. Brass is a symbol of judgment. In Revelation we read of Jesus, with feet of brass, going forth in judgment (1:15). Here is a beautiful picture of God's judgment for man's sin: Christ on the cross. No wonder Jesus said, "As Moses lifted up the serpent in the wilderness, even so must the Son of Man be lifted up" (John 3:14).

God's remedy for us is absolute. Moses didn't say, "Here is one way. But if you don't want to look at the serpent on the pole, then try some liniment or some ointment." No! There was only one remedy for sin for the Israelites and only one remedy for us: "Look and live." This remedy never failed. Everyone who looked was healed. God's remedy was easy. Look and live.

> There was only one remedy for sin for the Israelites and only one remedy for us: "Look and live."

They didn't have to work for their cure, pay for their cure, or earn their cure through their own good works. They didn't have to be erudite or educated or experienced. The cure was so simple a little child could receive it. Just look . . . and live! And one other thing, they had to look for themselves. No one could look for another. There is no clearer picture of the way of salvation in all the Bible than in this beautiful picture of Christ in Numbers, a bronze serpent on a pole.

Jesus still says, "Look at Me and live." Anyone can look. You can look. I can look. You don't need to have social standing or political power to look. It does not require an educational pedigree. It doesn't demand moral excellence. The vilest sinner can look to Jesus and live. To look to Jesus in faith seems so simple, yet it is all God requires. Jesus shows up in the book of Numbers to remind us of His sacrifice on the cross for you and me. Yes, just as Moses lifted up the serpent in the wilderness, so was the Son of God, our Savior, the Lord Jesus Christ lifted up on a Roman cross. And the good news is, everyone who looks to Him lives . . . and lives forever.

5   FINDING JESUS IN DEUTERONOMY

He Is the Manna in the Wilderness

The LORD your God led you all the way these forty years in the wilderness, to humble you and test you, to know what was in your heart, whether you would keep His commandments or not. So He humbled you, allowed you to hunger, and fed you with manna . . . that He might make you know that man shall not live by bread alone; but . . . every word that proceeds from the mouth of the LORD.

—DEUTERONOMY 8:2–3

*F*our of the first five books of the Bible, the books of Moses, have to do with Israel and their forty years of wilderness wanderings. Paul related that "all these things happened to them as examples, and they were written for our admonition" (1 Corinthians 10:11). Every experience they had in the wilderness holds a lesson for those of us living in this dispensation of grace. Knowing this and pointing to the sustaining manna that fell from heaven each morning, the Lord Jesus revealed, "Moses did not give you the bread from heaven, but My Father gives you the true bread from heaven. For the bread of God is He who comes down from heaven and gives life to the world. . . . I am the bread of life. He who comes to Me shall never hunger" (John 6:32–35).

It only took a month after passing through the Red Sea for the food supplies to run out for the hundreds of thousands of Israelites traveling toward their promised land. Hunger set in. The kids were crying. The parents were complaining, questioning Moses' leadership. He must have been feeling like Philip on the Galilean mountainside when Jesus asked him, "Where shall we buy bread, that these may eat?" (v. 5). Just when Moses was desperate for a solution, God was there with a promise: "I will rain bread from heaven for you. And the people shall go out and gather a certain quota every day" (Exodus 16:4). And true to His word, for the next forty years, God fed His people in this way . . . every morning . . . all they needed.

This miraculous provision was called "the bread of heaven" (Psalm 78:24). Similar to the dew that covered the ground, it was fine and flake-like. The Israelites gathered it each morning, ground it, then pounded it into cakes, which were then baked. It tasted like "wafers made with honey" (Exodus 16:31). Manna was not a product of this world cultivated or manufactured by human hands. It was supernatural. It was a gift that came down from heaven. It had to be gathered daily as it was only good for that day's supply. If it was left over until the next day, it became corrupt with worms, with the exception of the Sabbath when the preceding day brought a double portion. The manna never ran out. There was an inexhaustible supply that fed over two million people every day for forty years until they crossed over the Jordan River and began to feast on the milk and honey of Canaan, their promised land.

There is so much behind those words of Christ, "I am the bread of life" (John 6:35). He is the true manna that came down from the Father to sustain us and give us life. The manna of the wilderness demonstrated to the world that we have a God who cares and provides for us. Just as the manna arrived supernaturally, so did Jesus Christ. He miraculously came down from heaven; was planted into the womb of a young, Jewish virgin; and appeared in a Middle Eastern stable one star-filled night. Just as the manna had to be gathered and eaten by each individual, so each of us individually must receive Jesus by faith through being born again. Just as this manna was needed day by day, our Lord prayed, "Give us this day our *daily* bread" (Matthew 6:11, emphasis added). Yesterday's victories never suffice for today's commitment. With Jesus, God's mercies are "new every morning" (Lamentations 3:23). And just as the manna never ran out, in Christ there is an inexhaustible supply of love, joy, peace, and all the remaining fruit of the Spirit.

> Yesterday's victories never suffice for today's commitment.

Yes, "all these things happened to them as examples, and they were written for our admonition" (1 Corinthians 10:11). Like our Jewish forefathers of the faith, we, too, look to God for our sustenance and our salvation, which is freely and supernaturally provided for us in the One who called Himself "the Bread of Life." Every piece of manna digested by the children of Israel was the voice of God, saying that He is the Bread that "comes down from heaven and gives life to the world. . . . He who comes to Me shall never hunger" (John 6:33, 35). Jesus is in all the Bible, and we find Him here in Deuteronomy. He is the Bread of Life.

6 FINDING JESUS IN JOSHUA

He Is the Scarlet Cord out Rahab's Window

"When we come into the land, you bind this line of scarlet cord in the window through which you let us down." . . . *Then she said, "According to your words, so be it." And she sent them away, and they departed. And she bound the scarlet cord in the window. . . . And Joshua spared Rahab the harlot, . . . because she hid the messengers whom Joshua sent to spy out Jericho.*

—JOSHUA 2:18, 21; 6:25

*A*fter four decades of waiting, the time had finally come. Moses was dead. Joshua and the people of Israel were encamped on the east side of the Jordan opposite Jericho. On the threshold of entering the promised land, Joshua was fully aware that an immediate confrontation would ensue. Jericho, the well-fortified city in the Jordan valley, was the first of many battles that initiated the conquest of Canaan. Joshua sent two spies undercover into Jericho to bring back a reconnaissance report. Their cover about to be exposed, they were protected and hidden by one of the town prostitutes, Rahab. She lowered them over the wall with a rope through the window of her home so that they could safely return to Joshua with their report. They relayed that the walls were sixty feet high and thirty feet wide around the city. They couldn't be scaled over, skirted around, or tunneled under. They also brought news of Rahab. They had left her a scarlet cord to be hung from her window so that when the Israelites defeated Jericho, she and her household would be spared when the scarlet cord identified their home.

We all know the story well. The Israelites marched around the city of Jericho for seven days. As the residents of Jericho watched, hundreds of thousands of Israelites surrounded their city, marching around it. All of Jericho was terrified. Joshua was coming. Judgment was coming. Chaos and confusion ran rampant through the streets. Except for one home. Rahab was watching also. But she felt no fear. She had heard what God had done for the Israelites on the other side of the Jordan and professed, "The LORD your God, He is God in heaven above and on earth beneath" (Joshua 2:11). It is one thing to believe He is God in heaven, but another to believe He is in control of "earth beneath." As an expression of her faith, she hung the scarlet cord out her window. She was looking for her salvation. Through the Israelites' faith and by a miracle of God, the walls of Jericho fell down flat, and the city was destroyed. But not Rahab.

When Rahab said yes to the God of Israel and, by faith, hung the scarlet cord out her window, it set in motion her deliverance. God in heaven knew about a cross that she knew nothing about. The blood was shed on that cross "before the foundation of the world" (1 Peter 1:20). God saw that coming cross and the salvation it so

> When Rahab said yes to the God of Israel . . . it set in motion her deliverance.

perfectly promised and looked down on the faith of that sinful woman and saved her by His blood. As a declaration of her faith, Rahab hung the scarlet cord out her window so that when judgment came and the walls fell down flat, there was one conspicuous part of that wall that judgment could not touch . . . because of that scarlet cord.

Rahab was saved when judgment came (Joshua 6:22–25). She took her place among the Israelites in the family of God's people. The old things had passed, and all became new for her. She lived among the children of Israel and married a man named Salmon. They had a son and named him Boaz. Yes, the same Boaz who became the husband of Ruth and the father of Obed, who later gave birth to Jesse the father of David, who became the king. And as though this were not honor enough for Rahab, she is listed in the lineage of Jesus Himself in Matthew 1:5. She is the incarnate truth of 2 Corinthians 5:17: "If anyone is in Christ, he is a new creation; old things have passed away; behold, all things have become new."

There is a scarlet cord that is easily seen woven throughout the fabric of the Old Testament from Genesis to Malachi. All the foreshadowing, all the types, all the prophecies, and all the pictures look forward to and point toward the consummating sacrifice of the Lord Jesus Christ. The scarlet cord is really the story of the sacrifice of our Lord and His own rich, red, royal blood—blood shed to purchase our redemption. And for all of us who, like Rahab, hang this scarlet cord, by faith, from the windows of our hearts, it will mean deliverance and a new life for us, just as it did for her. Jesus is right here in the middle of one of the most well-known Old Testament stories, the fall of Jericho. He is, indeed, the scarlet cord hung from Rahab's window.

7 FINDING JESUS IN JUDGES

He Is Our Faithful Judge

And when the LORD raised up judges for them, the LORD was with the judge and delivered them out of the hand of their enemies all the days of the judge; for the LORD was moved to pity by their groaning because of those who oppressed them and harassed them.

—JUDGES 2:18

*T*he book of Judges—beginning after the death of Joshua and extending to the reign of King Saul—was a transition time for the children of Israel. This snapshot in their long history depicts a time when they forgot God and pursued the pagan gods of Canaan. The author comes right to the point, declaring, "Another generation arose after them who did not know the LORD nor the work which He had done for Israel. . . . They forsook the LORD God of their fathers, who had brought them out of the land of Egypt" (Judges 2:10, 12). During this period God repeatedly raised up a series of judges, among them Gideon and Samson, whom He appointed to defend His people, point them back to the Lord, and restore the peace among them.

More than any other book in the Bible, Judges describes the times in which we are living today. The last phrase in this book speaks volumes about their situation and ours: "Everyone did what was right in his own eyes" (Judges 21:25). Like our Jewish forefathers in the faith, we are living in a world today where relativism is rampant and *everyone does what is right in his or her own eyes.* What, just a few years ago, slithered down the dark back alleys of our culture now parades proudly down the main street of virtually every city, town, and village in America.

The people of God in Judges continually repeated a pathetic pattern. They would rebel against their God and His Word. Then they would face judgment. This would be followed by God providing a judge—a deliverer—for them, which would then be followed by a time of repentance and restoration. But it never lasted. Soon the entire process would be repeated, over and over and over again, as is recorded in the twenty-one chapters of Judges. Written across this book of the Old Testament is the truth of Hebrews 12:6–7, "'For whom the LORD loves He chastens.' . . . If you endure chastening, God deals with you as with sons; for what son is there whom a father does not chasten?"

Judges is the story of the good news. Man falls into sin. God brings judgment. Man cries out to God for pardon. God delivers him. This is the story of Jesus. Here is Jesus in Judges. Here is grace abounding more than sin. The Israelites may have forgotten their God, but God did not—will not—forget

His people. In Judges, we can glimpse our own faithful Judge, the Lord Jesus Christ. This book is a living testimony of God's faithfulness: "If we are faithless, He remains faithful" (2 Timothy 2:13).

> The Israelites may have forgotten their God, but God did not—will not—forget His people.

The role of these judges, as the divinely appointed deliverers, points to the Judge who is yet to come, our Lord Jesus. His is the one court where ultimate and perfect justice will prevail. Those of us who have put our trust in Christ will one day stand before the "judgment seat of Christ" (2 Corinthians 5:10). Here our works will be judged, not our sins. Our sins were judged on the cross. One of the most beautiful aspects of this judgment of the saints is that "we have an Advocate with the Father, Jesus Christ the righteous" (1 John 2:1). Christ, our Judge and Advocate, will plead our case, and God cannot and will not see our sins through the blood of Jesus. On the other hand, those who never trusted in Christ as their personal Savior will stand before the "great white throne" (Revelation 20:11) where they will give an account for their lives, and the degree of their eternal punishment will be decided on.

In his New Testament letter, James warned, "The Judge is standing at the door!" (James 5:9). The Lord Jesus, our faithful Judge, used the same imagery when He said, "Behold, I

stand at the door and knock. If anyone hears My voice and opens the door, I will come into him and dine with him, and he with Me. To him who overcomes I will grant to sit with Me on My throne, as I also overcame and sat down with My Father on His throne" (Revelation 3:20–21).

We find Jesus walking through these chapters in Judges, personified and pictured in the lives of these faithful deliverers. He is, and will be, our faithful Judge. Ultimately, we can rest in the truth of Genesis 18:25, "Shall not the Judge of all the earth do right?"

8 FINDING JESUS IN RUTH

He Is Our Kinsman-Redeemer

Then Naomi said to [Ruth], "Blessed be he of the LORD, who has not forsaken His kindness to the living and the dead!" And Naomi said to her, "This man [Boaz] is a relation of ours, one of our close relatives."
—RUTH 2:20

*O*ne of the most descriptive and detailed pictures of Christ is found in the person of Boaz in the book of Ruth. Famine had come to Judea. There was no bread in Bethlehem, the "house of bread." So a man by the name of Elimelech took his wife, Naomi, and their two sons and fled to the land of Moab, settling there. In due time, the sons each married Moabite women. The Moabites were a race who had been born in incest and observed a false religion that was the very antithesis of the Jewish faith of Elimelech and his family. Over time, Naomi's husband died and also her two sons. She, having heard the famine had ended, was now determined to return to Bethlehem. She encouraged her two daughters-in-law to go back to their own people and their own gods. One of them did just that. The other, Ruth, clung to Naomi, entreating, "Wherever you go, I will go" (Ruth 1:16). And so, these two penniless widows began their journey to Bethlehem, knowing Ruth's past would be against her living as a destitute pagan outsider in the Jewish world of Judea.

Ruth found a menial job, retrieving the leftovers of the harvest, gleaning in the fields of Bethlehem. It was the custom of the day that the next of kin had not only the right (Leviticus 25:23–34) but the biblical responsibility (Deuteronomy 25:5–10) to redeem and restore an impoverished relative. Boaz was a near kinsman of Naomi's husband, Elimelech. He was also a wealthy landowner in whose very fields Ruth was gleaning. Such a kinsman-redeemer was known in Hebrew as a *goel* to his needy relatives.

This idea of *goel* is at the very heart of the Bible's teaching of redemption. Three requirements were associated with this one who had the ability to redeem. First, he had to have the right to do so. That is, he had to be a close blood relative. Second, he had to have the financial wherewithal, the power, to be able to redeem. After all, it is one thing to have the right to redeem, but quite another to have the power to do so. Finally, the *goel* had to be willing to redeem an impoverished relative. Let's consider Boaz. He had the right to redeem Naomi and Ruth. He was a near kinsman "of the family of Elimelech" (Ruth 2:1). He certainly had the power in that he was "a man of great wealth" (Ruth 2:1). And he was certainly willing, in that he had lost his heart and fallen in love with this Gentile girl, Ruth, whom he had seen gleaning in his fields.

The Lord Jesus Christ is our very own Boaz. He has the right to redeem us. When it came time to redeem us, He laid aside His own glory, left the splendors of heaven, and came down past solar systems and through measureless space to be planted in the womb of a young virgin girl and to be born in the very village Boaz once called home: Bethlehem. Jesus took on flesh, became as one of us, to meet the first requirement of the *goel*.

> The Lord Jesus Christ is our very own Boaz. He has the right to redeem us.

Jesus also has the power to redeem us. He is wealthy enough to pay redemption's price, the price of blood that He shed to purchase our redemption on Calvary's cross. Already possessing the right and the power to redeem us, all that was left was the will to do so, and Jesus willingly laid down His own life, dying our death so that we could live His life. I was Ruth. You were Ruth. We were born outside the family of God and separated from God in our sin. But we have a Kinsman-redeemer. The Lord Jesus Christ, our Boaz, rushed out to Golgotha, and now we can join the apostle Paul in saying, "In Him we have redemption through His blood, the forgiveness of sins, according to the riches of His grace" (Ephesians 1:7).

Few stories have such an incredible ending. The book of Ruth may have opened with three funerals, but it closes with a wedding. Ruth married Boaz, the lord of the harvest, her kinsman-redeemer. They had a son, Obed, who had a son named Jesse, who had a son named David, the shepherd, psalmist, king. Ruth, this former godless Moabite, became the great-grandmother of Israel's greatest king. She lived a beautiful life and left a lasting legacy, totally separated from her old life in Moab. The entire course of her life was determined by another person, Boaz. What a wonderful picture of you and me when we truly say to our Redeemer what Ruth said to Naomi: "Wherever you go, I will go; and wherever you lodge, I will lodge; your people shall be my people, and your God, my God" (Ruth 1:16). Today, Ruth lives on in history and in heaven, an example for us all, because of her very own kinsman-redeemer, Boaz. Yes, we find Jesus here in the middle of the book of Ruth. He is our Boaz, our very own Kinsman-Redeemer.

9 FINDING JESUS IN FIRST AND SECOND SAMUEL

He Is Our Trusted Prophet

So Samuel grew, and the LORD was with him and let none of his words fall to the ground. And all Israel from Dan to Beersheba knew that Samuel had been established as a prophet of the LORD.

—1 SAMUEL 3:19–20

*W*hen we arrive at the books of First and Second Samuel, we find a turning point in Israel's history. As discussed in chapter 7, after the death of Joshua, Israel was ruled by a series of judges who governed with no centralized authority over the nation. God would repeatedly raise up these individuals to deliver Israel from her enemies (Judges 2:16). Samuel was the last of these judges and pivoted the people away from the rule of judges to the reign of a series of kings. The first two of them, Saul and David, were anointed to kingship by Samuel himself. Simon Peter identified Samuel as not just the last of the judges but the first of the prophets (Acts 3:24). In his day, Samuel stood out as the undisputed and established "prophet of the LORD" (1 Samuel 3:19–20).

To this day, high on a hill on the northern outskirts of

Jerusalem, there stands a tall tower that can be seen for miles around in all directions. This tower marks the grave of the prophet Samuel. His life began as a miracle child when God heard the prayers of his godly mother and opened her barren womb to gift the world with the first and greatest of Israel's prophets. As would later be said of our Lord, Samuel "grew in stature, and in favor both with the LORD and men" (1 Samuel 2:26). When the Israelites ignored Samuel's warnings and insisted on an earthly king—rejecting God as their king—God gave them what they wanted. Though in the centuries to come, the Israelites would find that what they wanted was not what they needed. Samuel, led by God, anointed Saul as king of Israel. Later, after Saul began to turn away from God, the prophet anointed Israel's second king, David.

A prophet is best defined as one who speaks to men for God. In contrast, a priest is one who speaks to God for men. Samuel was the mouthpiece of God, thundering forth, "Thus saith the Lord" to the people of Israel for decades. As a prophet, he fulfilled three major functions:

1. He revealed God to the people.
2. He was God's official spokesman.

3. And he communicated to the people the valuable
    truths God desired for them to know and obey.

Thus the prophet stood before the people to reveal who
God is, what God says, and why God speaks.

Moses had earlier revealed that the Lord had spoken
to him, saying, "I will raise up for them a Prophet like you
from among their brethren, and will put My words in His
mouth, and He shall speak to them all that I command Him"
(Deuteronomy 18:18). Leaving no doubt as to whom the Lord
was speaking, Simon Peter, standing in Solomon's Portico,
said, "To you first, God, having raised up His Servant Jesus,
sent Him to bless you, in turning away every one of you from
your iniquities" (Acts 3:26).

Like Samuel, we find Jesus walking through the pages of
Scripture, fulfilling all three of the functions of a prophet:

1. *He revealed who God is to the people.* The night
    before His own crucifixion, gathered in the Upper
    Room on Mount Zion with His followers, Jesus
    revealed the Father to all of us when He said, "If
    you had known Me, you would have known My
    Father also; and from now on you know Him and
    have seen Him" (John 14:7). Philip interjected,
    "Lord, show us the Father" (v. 8). Jesus again

revealed the Father in no uncertain terms by responding, "Have I been with you so long, and yet you have not known Me, Philip? He who has seen Me has seen the Father" (v. 9).

2. *He was God's official spokesman.* So that there would be no doubt that He was the true Prophet from God, Jesus declared, "I have not spoken on My own authority; but the Father who sent Me gave Me a command, what I should say and what I should speak" (John 12:49). And again, in the Upper Room, He reaffirmed this truth, saying, "The words that I speak to you I do not speak on My own authority; but the Father who dwells in Me does the works" (John 14:10). Jesus, our trusted Prophet, came to reveal God to us and to speak God the Father's own words to us.

3. *He foretold and communicated the valuable truths God wanted us to know.* Jesus foretold the future. He told His disciples of His own pending death and resurrection (Matthew 17:22–23; 20:17–19). He told of Judas' betrayal and Peter's denial before they took place (John 13:18–30, 36–38). He predicted the coming of the Holy Spirit (John 16:7–15). And He prophesied of His own second coming (John 14:3).

The writer of Hebrews placed a bow on this wonderful truth by saying, "God, who at various times and in various ways spoke in time past to the fathers by the prophets, has in these last days spoken to us by His Son, whom He has appointed heir of all things" (1:1–2). Jesus, our trusted Prophet, is the greatest of all the prophets because in Him God came to be among us: "The Word became flesh and dwelt among us" (John 1:14).

10 FINDING JESUS IN KINGS AND CHRONICLES

He Is the Fire Coming Down from Heaven

When Solomon had finished praying, fire came down from heaven and consumed the burnt offering and the sacrifices; and the glory of the LORD filled the temple. And the priests could not enter the house of the LORD, because the glory of the LORD had filled the LORD's house. When all the children of Israel saw how the fire came down, and the glory of the LORD on the temple, they bowed their faces to the ground on the pavement, and worshiped and praised the LORD, saying, "For He is good, for His mercy endures forever."

—2 CHRONICLES 7:1–3

The book of Judges ends with these tragic words: "In those days there was no king in Israel; everyone did what was right in his own eyes" (Judges 21:25). The people began to demand of Samuel, the last of the judges and now well advanced in years, "a king to judge us like all the nations" (1 Samuel 8:5). And thus began, with Saul, the rule of the kings of Israel. The people would later learn a life lesson: what we want is not always what we need. God's intention was to reign over His chosen people. When their demand for a king displeased Samuel, the Lord reminded him that "they have not rejected you, but they have rejected Me, that I should not reign over them" (v. 7). The books of Kings and Chronicles begin with the reign of King David and conclude with the end of the time of the kings with the Babylonian captivity in 586 BC.

Repeatedly, throughout the Old Testament, we find Jesus appearing on the scene, manifesting Himself as fire from heaven. God judged the wicked cities of Sodom and Gomorrah by raining down fire upon them (Genesis 19:24). After forty years on the backside of a desert, Moses received his call to become the great emancipator of his people when the Lord spoke to him from the fire of a burning bush: "And the Angel of the LORD [the preincarnate Christ] appeared to him in a flame of fire from the midst of a bush. . . . And behold, the bush was burning with fire, but the bush was not consumed" (Exodus 3:2). Another of these more prominent appearances was in the wilderness wanderings when Christ came to lead His people each night as "a pillar of fire." Moses declared, "You, LORD, are among these people; that You, LORD, are seen face to face . . . and You go before them . . . in a pillar of fire by night" (Numbers 14:14).

Above all the other Old Testament scriptures, the books of Kings and Chronicles are laced throughout with these appearances of Jesus, walking through their chapters and manifesting as the fire coming down from heaven. We find

Jesus in Elijah's confrontation with the false prophets of Baal on Mount Carmel in 1 Kings 18 when we read, "'You call on the name of your gods, and I will call on the name of the LORD; and the God who answers by fire, He is God'.... Then the fire of the LORD fell and consumed the burnt sacrifice.... When all the people saw it, they fell on their faces; and they said, 'The LORD, He is God! The LORD, He is God!'" (vv. 24, 38–39). At the end of the great prophet Elijah's life as he was walking and talking with Elisha, "suddenly a chariot of fire appeared . . . and separated the two of them; and Elijah went up by a whirlwind into heaven" (2 Kings 2:11). Jesus showed up as fire once again when King David purchased the threshing floor on the summit of Mount Moriah, which would for centuries become the altar of sacrifice in the Jewish temple. Upon purchasing this prized possession, King David built an altar there and offered sacrifices, calling on the name of the Lord, and "He answered him from heaven by fire on the altar of burnt offering" (1 Chronicles 21:26). Decades later, when on that same exact spot, David's son King Solomon dedicated the magnificent Jewish temple, "fire came down from heaven and consumed the burnt offering and the sacrifices; and the glory of the LORD filled the temple" (2 Chronicles 7:1).

You and I may not be living in the times of the kings of Israel, but each of us will have our own personal experience of finding Jesus as a burning fire. Paul warned of a coming time of judgment when "each one's work will become clear; for the Day will declare it, because it will be revealed by fire; and the fire will test each one's work, of what sort it is. If anyone's work which he has built on it endures, he will receive a reward. If anyone's work is burned, he will suffer loss; but he himself will be saved, yet so as through fire" (1 Corinthians 3:13–15). Christ is a refining fire who will one day burn away all the impurities of our lives, and by His lovingkindness He will present us before His Father's throne "faultless before the presence of His glory with exceeding joy" (Jude v. 24). The entire Bible is about Jesus. Today, we are not led by pillars of fire or spoken to through the fire of a burning bush. We have something those Old Testament saints didn't have. We have the same Spirit that raised Christ from the dead living in us to guide us through life and to reveal God's way to us by His Spirit and through His Word. Yes, we find Jesus all through Kings and Chronicles. "Our God is a consuming fire" (Hebrews 12:29).

> Christ is a refining fire who will one day burn away all the impurities of our lives.

11   FINDING JESUS IN EZRA

He Is Our Faithful Scribe

Ezra . . . was a skilled scribe in the Law of Moses, which the LORD God of Israel had given. . . . For Ezra had prepared his heart to seek the Law of the LORD, and to do it.

—EZRA 7:6, 10

*F*ollowing the Babylonian exile, three prominent Jewish leaders returned to the devastated city of Jerusalem. Zerubbabel was assigned the task of leading in the rebuilding of the temple, which had been plundered and left in ruins. Nehemiah mobilized and motivated the Jewish exiles to rebuild the city's broken walls and burned gates that left it vulnerable to enemies. But it was the faithful scribe Ezra's task to accomplish the most important of the rebuilding assignments. Ezra pointed the people to God's Word and led in the crucial rebuilding of the spiritual integrity of the people of God. And, like all great leaders, he led by example: "Ezra had prepared his heart to seek the Law of the LORD, and to do it" (Ezra 7:10).

While we never read of a direct mention of the Messiah in Ezra, it is impossible to miss Jesus walking through these verses, manifesting Himself in the life of this faithful scribe.

As a scribe, Ezra revered and honored the holy Scriptures and sought not to simply know them but to put them in practice in his daily life. In like manner, Jesus loved the Scriptures and built His earthly life upon them. When, after His baptism, He was led into the wilderness to be tempted by Satan, He answered each attempt to sidetrack Him from His mission by saying, "It is written" (Matthew 4:4, 7, 10). Jesus stood on the Word of God and applied it to every detail of His life.

All of Scripture was given to us by "inspiration" of the Lord Himself (2 Timothy 3:16). *Inspiration* means the words are God's own words, and He gave them to man through men. Simon Peter said, "Holy men of God spoke as they were moved by the Holy Spirit" (2 Peter 1:21). Ironically, the identical Greek word translated here as "moved" appears in the accounts of Paul's shipwreck recorded in Acts 27. There came a fierce storm and the sailors on board, unable to guide or steer the ship because of the strong winds, simply let the winds take the ship wherever they blew it (Acts 27:15, 17). Just as the sailors were active on the ship, yet had relinquished control over where it would go, so it was with the Bible's writers. In a very real sense, the writings were not their own. God expressed this very point to Jeremiah, saying, "I have put My words in your mouth" (Jeremiah 1:9). The Scripture never originated with men; it originated with the Lord Himself. The writers' personalities and styles are unique to them, but it was God who moved them to write by His Spirit, the same Spirit who raised Christ from the dead. Ezra grasped this truth and submitted himself, like our Lord when He was encased in human flesh, to these truths.

We also find Jesus reflected in Ezra as the faithful scribe wept over Jerusalem, just as our Lord would weep over the same city four and a half centuries later. Ezra poured out his heart with tears of remorse for the wasted years of Israel's rebellion (Ezra 10:1). This is reminiscent of our Lord's actions on what should have been a grand and glorious day, as He rode into the Holy City amid the cheers and hosannas of the adoring throngs. Jesus should have been smiling from ear to ear and waving as He passed down that Palm Sunday road, but instead He was weeping: "Now as He drew near, He saw the city and wept over it, saying, 'If you had known, even you, especially in this your day, the things that make for your peace! But now they are hidden from your eyes'" (Luke 19:41–42).

Ezra's call for repentance and moral reform found their ultimate fulfillment in Jesus Christ. In His Sermon on the Mount, Jesus laid forth the original intent of the Lawgiver Himself. Repeatedly we hear Him say, "You have heard . . . But I say to you . . ." (Matthew 5:21–48). For example, Jesus stated that we have

> Ezra's call for repentance and moral reform found their ultimate fulfillment in Jesus Christ.

heard we should not commit adultery. And then He added, "But I say to you that whoever looks at a woman to lust for her has already committed adultery with her in his heart" (v. 28). Jesus didn't dispute what was written in the law of Moses; rather, He gave us the original intent of the Lawgiver Himself. After all, *He* was the author. Jesus made the law a matter of the heart.

Ezra, like Jesus, gave the people of God something that would endure through the centuries to come. He organized the chosen people around the Torah, the Word of God. Until this very day, this is the distinguishing mark of the Jewish people—not geography or national origin—but adherence to God's Word, the sacred Torah. This is what sustained them through Roman persecution, worldwide dispersion, the Spanish Inquisition, the Russian pogroms, the Polish ghettos, and the Nazi death camps. God's Word, both living in the person of Christ and written in the holy Scriptures, is alive and well. When we see Ezra, there is a real sense in which we see our own faithful Scribe, the Lord Jesus Christ, for "in the beginning was the Word, and the Word was with God, and the Word was God. . . . And the Word became flesh and dwelt among us, and we beheld His glory, the glory as of the only begotten of the Father, full of grace and truth" (John 1:1, 14). We find Jesus walking through these verses of Ezra. He was and is and forever will be our faithful Scribe.

12 FINDING JESUS IN NEHEMIAH

He Is the Rebuilder of Our Broken Walls

Then the king said to me, "What do you request?" . . . And I said to the king, "If it pleases the king, and if your servant has found favor in your sight, I ask that you send me to Judah, to the city of my fathers' tombs, that I may rebuild it."

—NEHEMIAH 2:4–5

*N*ehemiah lived some 2,500 years ago, and he "wrote the book" on rebuilding. God recorded it for us and placed it in the Bible for all posterity. Nehemiah was neither a preacher nor a prophet. He was a civil servant, an ordinary guy who applied some universal principles that enabled him to rebuild a broken city and, in the process, a lot of broken hopes. His story unfolds years after the Babylonians destroyed the city of Jerusalem and took captives away into Babylon. They demolished the temple, broke down the ancient walls, and burned the city gates. For years, the Holy City lay in ruins. Motivated by his passion to restore Jerusalem to its former glory, he took it upon himself to return, encourage the remnant that remained, and rebuild the city's broken walls. In just fifty-two days this amazing feat was accomplished (Nehemiah 6:15). But not without tremendous opposition from without and also from within.

Conflict will tear your team apart—whether it is at home, in the office, on the court, or even in the church. Unresolved conflicts can do irreparable damage. Nehemiah, chapter 5, finds the Jews faced with the very real possibility that the wall might not be rebuilt due to some conflicts that had arisen between members of Nehemiah's own team. Long before any of the modern motivational gurus wrote on conflict resolution, Nehemiah employed four essential, and now time-tested, elements to resolve their conflicts and enable the rebuilding of the broken walls.

First, Nehemiah revealed to us that *there is a time to back off*. Nehemiah began by backing off. And there was a wise reason to do so. He had, in his own words, become "very angry" (Nehemiah 5:6). He was wise enough to know that when this happens, the best thing we can do is back off and give some "serious thought" (v. 7) to the situation. This phrase in our English Bibles translates two Hebrew words meaning "to counsel or give advice" and "the inner man, the heart." Nehemiah was literally saying, "I backed off and listened to my heart. I took counsel with my heart." And in so doing he found a course of action that ultimately led his people back on the walls and back to the business of rebuilding.

After backing off, Nehemiah next revealed *there is a*

time to stand up. He boldly stood up and confronted those he believed to be wrong and whose actions had initiated the conflict (vv. 7–9). Conflict resolution never means simply backing off and always giving in at any cost. Jesus, in the Sermon on the Mount, pronounced a blessing on the "peace-makers," not the "peace lovers" (Matthew 5:9). There are times we must stand up and make peace with others.

Third, Nehemiah revealed to us that *there is a time to give in.* He allowed others to save face and knew it was far more important to give in on a few nonessentials (Nehemiah 5:10–11). It is always best in our own relationships to lose a few little, insignificant battles in order to win a much bigger war. Nehemiah was not showing weakness by allowing others to have their way in nonessentials. He was showing strength. Too many conflicts are left unresolved because some people insist they must win every little argument and point.

Finally, we see in Nehemiah that *there is a time to reach out.* He built bridges, not barriers. With tender persuasion he reached out and pleaded with the people to move past their differences in view of everyone's higher calling (vv. 8–13). And what was the result of this fourfold approach? "All the assembly said, 'Amen!' and praised the LORD. Then the people did according to this promise" (v. 13). Shalom returned!

Can you see Jesus walking through these pages in

Nehemiah? You and I were in conflict with Him. We had gone our own way, we had "all sinned" and fallen short of His plan for us (Romans 3:23). So what did He do? He backed off. In His darkest hour, see Him beneath those old, gnarled olive trees in Gethsemane's garden. In "serious thought," He backed off and took counsel with His own heart. Then He stood up. See Him before Caiaphas, the high priest; Herod, the puppet king; and Pilate, the Roman governor. When asked if He was the Son of God, Jesus boldly replied, "You rightly say that I am" (Luke 22:70). Next, He gave in. He was not pushed, shoved, and kicked up the Via Dolorosa. He gave in and willingly went, "led as a lamb to the slaughter" (Isaiah 53:7). Finally, Jesus reached out. Suspended between heaven and earth on a cross, with arms outstretched, Jesus reached out, imploring us all to be "reconciled to God" (Romans 5:10). Yes, we find Jesus in Nehemiah as He is about the task of rebuilding our own broken walls.

During the rebuilding process, Nehemiah had a rallying point for his entire team. He kept a trumpeter always close and constantly by his side. His instructions were, "Wherever you hear the sound of the trumpet, rally to us there. Our God will fight for us" (Nehemiah 4:20). All across our world today, there are all

> We find Jesus in Nehemiah as He is about the task of rebuilding our own broken walls.

kinds of men and women aiding in Christ's own rebuilding process. They are preachers, missionaries, teachers, laborers, laypersons—and they are scattered all along the wall. In some places, the ranks are thin. But we all have our own Commander in Chief, the Lord Jesus Christ, and He is the rallying point for all of us under His service. One day we will hear His trumpeter give the final trumpet sound. We will lay down our tools, leave our workstations, and rally around Him when He comes to receive us as His own.

The Bible is the Jesus book. It is all about Him. And He is right here, in the book of Nehemiah, the Rebuilder of our broken walls.

13 FINDING JESUS IN ESTHER

He Is Our Mordecai

Mordecai had brought up Hadassah, that is, Esther, his uncle's daughter, for she had neither father nor mother. . . . For Mordecai the Jew was second to King Ahasuerus, and was great among the Jews and well received by the multitude of his brethren, seeking the good of his people and speaking peace to all his countrymen.

—ESTHER 2:7; 10:3

*M*ost of us have an appendage that stays right by our side during the daylight hours and not too far away even when we are fast asleep. We have developed such a dependency on this appendage that there is hardly a part of our lives in which it is not involved. I am speaking of our smartphones. We talk on them, text on them, and tweet on them. We schedule on them and get our news from them. We do our banking on them and pay our bills on them. We watch the weather on them and even awaken each day to an alarm on them. But one of the greatest features on my own smartphone is the camera, which takes better pictures than any camera I have ever owned. If you are like me, you have thousands of pictures stored on your phone—pictures of kids, grandkids, vacations, friends, and scores of other memories treasured up for you somewhere in the iCloud. We love showing our friends pictures of our kids. Did you know that God delights in the very same thing? He loves showing us pictures of His Son from every possible angle and in every possible place. As we walk through the books of the Bible, God shows us different pictures of His Son, Jesus. Here, in the book of Esther, we find a beautiful picture of Jesus in the life of a man by the name of Mordecai.

The book of Esther is the only book in the Bible where the name of God is not mentioned—not once. And, ironically, when the Dead Sea Scrolls were discovered in 1948, all the books of the Old Testament were found in the scrolls . . . except for this book, which bears the name of Esther. On the surface, it appears to be about a beautiful Jewish girl who miraculously became the queen of Persia and, in so doing, was able to heroically save the lives of the Jews who dwelt there. However, while Esther is under the spotlight on center stage, the real hero of the drama is standing off stage, in the shadows of the wings. His name is Mordecai, and in so many ways he presents a beautiful picture of Jesus.

While both Ezra and Nehemiah were taken up with the remnant of Jews who left Persia to return to Jerusalem and rebuild the ancient city, Esther is the story of the Jews who remained in Persia. It is the personal account of how God providentially worked through the lives of Esther and her adoptive father, Mordecai, a low-level worker in the king's court, to protect His chosen people living in a pagan land. The unfolding events in Esther are like reading a Jeffrey Archer novel with a twist at every turn. There are intrigue, political manipulations, death threats, plot twists, and, of course, romance. When the story opens, Esther has been elevated to the position of queen by a beauty contest of sorts. In the words of Mordecai, God exalted her "for such a time as this" (Esther 4:14). Meanwhile, Haman, an egomaniacal court official, planned to exterminate the Jews and see Mordecai hung from the gallows. Through a miraculous set of events, Haman's plot was exposed, and he found himself hanging from the very rope he had reserved for Mordecai.

Throughout this narrative, time and again, we find Mordecai, behind the scenes, orchestrating deliverance for Esther and, ultimately, all the Jews. With his humble spirit, Mordecai presents to us a beautiful picture of Christ. And, similar to Jesus, it was Mordecai's own initiatives that saved and restored his people in days of darkness and distress. Mordecai's adoption of Esther is a reminder to us of our adoption into the family of God—a gift given to us through no merit or effort of our own. We see how he found Esther and not how she found

> With his humble spirit, Mordecai presents to us a beautiful picture of Christ.

him, reminding us that it is the Holy Spirit who does the seeking and that Christ is the One who found us, not we who found Him. The book of Esther ends with an account of "the greatness of Mordecai" (Esther 10:2). We see Jesus in this man who tenderly raised his orphaned relative, who faithfully served his king, who so consistently obeyed his God, and who was then elevated to a place of greatness. There is coming a day when Christ shall rule from the throne of David in a land of perfect peace. Until then may "the peace of God rule in your hearts" by faith (Colossians 3:15).

To this very day our Jewish friends read the book of Esther every year as they celebrate the festival of Purim. Even though the name of God is never mentioned in Esther, He is there in every verse, and we find Jesus Himself beautifully reflected in the life of Mordecai.

14   FINDING JESUS IN JOB

He Is Our Redeemer Who Ever Lives

For I know that my Redeemer lives, and He shall stand at last on the earth; and after my skin is destroyed, this I know, that in my flesh I shall see God, whom I shall see for myself, and my eyes shall behold, and not another. How my heart yearns within me!

—JOB 19:25–27

*A*t one point or another, most all of us have wondered silently what Job asked aloud: "If a man dies, shall he live again?" (Job 14:14). In other words, is this all there is? Are we simply here today, gone tomorrow, and then . . . nothing else? Or is there a life beyond this physical one?

God has instilled within the human heart a longing for a life beyond this earthly existence. Ancient cave dwellers depicted this hope in paintings etched inside their caves. The pharaohs of Egypt were buried within their great pyramids alongside weapons, eating utensils, and even servants— evidence that they, too, believed in a life beyond this existence. Native American Indians buried their dead believing they would live again in their "happy hunting grounds." Clearly our great God has supernaturally implanted within the human spirit a longing for a life beyond the grave.

Further fueling today's interest in life after death are the recurring accounts of "near-death experiences." Every few years, a new bestselling book hits the shelves describing someone's "death" and what that person experienced before returning to the body. These books have sold millions and resulted in more than one motion picture. Clearly, Job's question "sells" in our world today.

"If a man dies, shall he live again?" Job answered his own question, pointing to the coming Redeemer, the Lord Jesus Christ, with an emphatic, "Yes!" Listen to his confident confirmation: "I know that my Redeemer lives . . . and after my skin is destroyed . . . I shall see God" (Job 19:25–26).

These words came from the lips and pen of a man who had just lost his job, his health, his wealth, his friends, and, most of all, his family. Job did not say, "I think . . ." or, "I wish . . ." Nor did he say, "I hope . . ." Job's answer was *positive*. He was rock-solid certain. There were no "ifs" or "buts" about it. He knew that his Redeemer lived. Affirming the confidence of Job, the apostle John added, "These things I have written to you who believe in the name of the Son of God, that you may know that you have eternal life" (1 John 5:13). Your Bible was written to you so that you would have and hold to the positive assurance that not only is there

> Job's answer was positive. . . . He knew that his Redeemer lived.

another life more than a million times a million longer than this one, but you will spend it with Job's Redeemer, our Lord Jesus.

Job's answer was not only positive, it was *pointed*. He indicated that he would see his Redeemer after the destruction of his own fleshly body. We have previously seen Jesus, our Redeemer, walking through the pages of Ruth as He was—foreshadowed in the life of Boaz—our Kinsman-Redeemer. So, in essence, Job said, "I have lost everything. So what if death comes my way? I know that my Redeemer lives and that in the end He'll restore me. He lives, and I will live again also."

Outside the Damascus Gate and down Nablus Road in Jerusalem to this very day there is a beautiful garden, and in it lies a famous tomb. But there are many famous tombs in the world today. The pyramids in Egypt hold the bodies of the pharaohs. In Westminster Abbey lie the remains of Browning, Tennyson, Livingston, and others. In Mecca you can find the tomb of Mohammad. All those tombs are famous for who is inside. But the Garden Tomb in Jerusalem is famous for the One it doesn't contain. Job's answer is pointed: "I know that my Redeemer lives!"

Finally, Job's answer is intensely *personal*. He said it is "*my* Redeemer" who lives. Can you embrace that little one-syllable, two-letter, personal pronoun—"my"? If so, you will

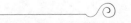

find Jesus here in the book of Job, your very own personal Redeemer who lives forever. In the midst of his great difficulties, Job's source of delight was seeing God in the next life. Job knew, and we can know, that heaven is a wonderful place. We will never see a hospital there, because there will be no more sickness. We will see no more funeral homes, because there will be no more death. We will never see or sense the need for any more counseling centers, because there will be no more depression, heartache, or mental illness. We will never see a police car, because there will be no more crime. Whatever it may be that takes the joy out of life will be gone forever for those who can say with Job, "I know that my Redeemer lives."

We find Jesus here in the middle of the book of Job. He is our Redeemer who ever lives. "If a man dies, shall he live again?" Yes, and those who have placed their faith and trust in Christ, our Redeemer, will see Him and live forever with Him in heaven. For Job, and for all of us believers, death is not about leaving home . . . it is about going home.

15 FINDING JESUS IN PSALMS

He Is Our Shepherd

The LORD is my shepherd; I shall not want. He makes me to lie down in green pastures; He leads me beside the still waters.

—PSALM 23:1–2

Virtually every educated mind in the English-speaking world has heard the words of this psalm of King David. These words to our loving Shepherd have been spoken by many a soldier under a star-filled sky, during a dark night in a foxhole on some faraway battlefield. These are the words whose syllables have been formed by, and whispered through, the lips of many while dying on a bed of affliction. These are the very words, like a lullaby for fear, that have brought hope and peace to millions across the centuries.

When, in a Galilean setting, Jesus said, "I am the good shepherd. The good shepherd gives His life for the sheep" (John 10:11), every hearer's mind must have raced back to these words of the psalmist: "The LORD is my shepherd" (Psalm 23:1). One of the clearest pictures of Jesus in the Old Testament is here in this old and oft-repeated psalm. The first five words hold the key and form the foundation of the entire chapter. "The . . . LORD . . . is . . . my . . . shepherd."

Once sealed in our hearts, these words speak volumes about our own relationship with this good Shepherd.

Note the first two words, "The Lord." The scripture does not say, "*A* Lord is my shepherd." It says, "*The* Lord is my shepherd." There is no other Lord. He is *preeminent*. If you speak of Washington, I can speak of Lincoln. If you speak of Beethoven, I can speak of Handel. If you speak of Alexander, I can speak of Napoleon. But when it comes to Christ, He stands alone. He has no peer. There is only one Lord.

Only the records of heaven have recorded how many martyrs have laid down their lives and met their deaths because they insisted on the first two words of this psalm, "The Lord." They gave their lives to proclaim the truth: Jesus is the one and only Lord.

David continued, "The Lord *is* my shepherd." Oh, the depth of meaning of this little two-letter word. This good Shepherd, Jesus, is with me right now. This is not past tense. It does not say, "The Lord *was* my shepherd." It is not future tense. It does not say, "The Lord *will be* my shepherd." He is not only preeminent, He is *present*—"*The* Lord *is* my shepherd." He is with us at this present moment to meet our immediate needs.

But there is more. The psalmist said, "The Lord is *my* shepherd." Jesus is intensely *personal*. There is a huge difference between saying, "The Lord is *a* shepherd" and saying,

"The LORD is *my* shepherd." What a difference comes to life's circumstances and situations with that little word *my*! We may hear of someone's child who is deathly sick and have compassion and feel sorrow. But what a vast difference it makes if it is "my" child. This is not just any shepherd of

> There is a huge difference between saying, "The LORD is *a* shepherd" and saying, "The LORD is *my* shepherd."

whom David speaks. This is *my* shepherd. You are not simply some insignificant speck of protoplasm in this vast array of solar systems. The fact that the God of this universe is concerned about you and me personally gives purpose and meaning to our brief sojourn here on this small planet, suspended in the vastness of the immeasurable universe. Say it softly and think on this wonderful truth—"The LORD is *my* shepherd."

One thousand years after David penned these words, Jesus made it clearly known He was the One the psalmist spoke of, saying, "I am the good shepherd. The good shepherd gives His life for the sheep" (John 10:11). We find Jesus, our Shepherd-Savior here in the Psalms.

We find that Jesus is not only preeminent, present, and personal, but He is also *protective*. "The LORD is my *shepherd*." One of the primary tasks of a shepherd is to protect his sheep. Without a good shepherd, the sheep could not

find their way to water or to other of life's necessities. The shepherd keeps a constant vigil, watching for wild animals or other dangers that might harm his sheep. A good shepherd also goes after the sheep that strays from the fold. Who could ever forget the story Jesus told of the lost sheep in Luke 15? Without a shepherd, sheep are virtually helpless. They cannot find their way through treacherous mountain passes or run fast enough to escape a predator, nor are they strong enough to defend themselves. Sheep are not prepared for flight or fight. Just as sheep need their shepherd, so do we need ours. Yes, "The LORD is my *shepherd*."

To this very day Bedouin shepherds can be seen on the hillsides of Judea walking with their sheep along the mountain paths. They are always in front of the sheep, never behind them. That is because unlike cattlemen with their cattle, shepherds never drive their sheep. Shepherds lead and the sheep follow. Our Lord will never force us or drive us against our will. He leads us, and all we have to do is follow.

As we journey through God's Word together, we are finding Jesus in every book of the Bible. No clearer picture of Him is found than here in the book of Psalms. He is our Shepherd. From His own lips come these poignant words, "My sheep hear My voice, and I know them, and they follow Me" (John 10:27). Are you listening? Are you following?

16 FINDING JESUS IN PROVERBS AND ECCLESIASTES

He Is Our Wisdom

Wisdom is the principal thing. Therefore get wisdom. And in all your getting, get understanding.

—PROVERBS 4:7

*F*or God gives wisdom and knowledge and joy to a man who is good in His sight" (Ecclesiastes 2:26). King Solomon is purported to be the wisest man who ever lived. He left us the Old Testament books of Proverbs and Ecclesiastes. Wisdom is the common thread woven through the words of these books. In the thirty-one chapters of Proverbs, we find the words *wise* or *wisdom* 113 times and in Ecclesiastes' twelve brief chapters we find these words 49 times. Wisdom is the theme that permeates and penetrates every page of these "Books of Wisdom." The apostle Paul revealed that Christ "became for us wisdom from God" (1 Corinthians 1:30). Even more explicitly, he referred to Christ as "the wisdom of God" (v. 24). We find Jesus here in Proverbs and Ecclesiastes. He is our wisdom.

We live in a world where knowledge is literally at our fingertips and exploding at an exponential pace. The Internet brings to everyone instant information of global events in real time. Many of today's textbooks are obsolete and out of date before the print is even dry. With just the click of a mouse, we have access to more knowledge through numerous computer search engines than at any time in history.

Yet wisdom seems practically nonexistent. Lives are in shambles. Position, power, and prosperity have not brought the peace and purpose they promised. There is a stark difference between knowledge and wisdom. *Knowledge* is the accumulation of facts. With dedication and determination, anyone can accumulate facts. What we need today is *wisdom*: the ability to take those facts, discern them, and put them into practice to address our needs in real-life situations.

Before Solomon ever penned Proverbs and Ecclesiastes, at not yet twenty years of age, he was about to be crowned king of Israel. It would be no small task to follow in the steps of his father, King David, one of the most dynamic and successful leaders in all human history. But when God asked Solomon a rather pointed question, "What shall I give you?" (1 Kings 3:5), the young man had the right answer. His priorities were in the right order. He didn't have to ponder or think long and hard about his answer. Right away, he requested, "Give to Your servant an understanding heart . . . that I may discern between good and evil" (v. 9). Solomon's desire was for the wisdom that is from above, not the wisdom of this world, so his simple request was for wisdom. Years later, when penning one of his proverbs, Solomon wrote, "Wisdom is the principal thing. Therefore get wisdom" (Proverbs 4:7).

> Solomon's desire was for the wisdom that is from above, not the wisdom of this world.

Unfortunately, in the midst of unrestrained power, Solomon's focus began to ever so slowly change. When he became an old man, bitterness filled his heart. He wrote Ecclesiastes to show us the folly of many of the things we deem so important or even essential—such things as learning, laughter, liquor, luxury, and lust. Then he arrived at his ultimate conclusion, "Vanity of vanities . . . all is vanity" (Ecclesiastes 12:8). The last chapter of Ecclesiastes paints a picture of an old man whose heart could no longer hear from God and so his final appeal to us was this: "Remember now your Creator in the days of your youth, before the difficult days come" (v. 1). Solomon concluded Ecclesiastes with what he called "the conclusion of the whole matter."

And his final word: "For God will bring every work into judgment, including every secret thing, whether good or evil" (v. 14). Truth always wins in the end. And Jesus is "the Truth" and the "wisdom of God."

Christ Jesus *is* our wisdom. James, in the New Testament, said that this heavenly wisdom is "from above" (James 3:17) and offered this invitation: "If any of you lacks wisdom, let him ask of God, who gives to all liberally and without reproach, and it will be given to him" (James 1:5). Wisdom is God's own supernatural gift, given to any and all who simply ask for it. The apostle Paul acknowledged this very fact while praying for the believers in Ephesus. He prayed "that the God of our Lord Jesus Christ, the Father of glory, may give to you the spirit of wisdom and revelation in the knowledge of Him" (Ephesians 1:17). A thousand years earlier Solomon acknowledged this when he wrote, "The LORD gives wisdom" (Proverbs 2:6).

A key to abiding in this wisdom from above is repeated throughout Proverbs as Solomon wrote, "The fear of the LORD is the beginning of wisdom" (Proverbs 9:10). The door to receiving this supernatural wisdom is opened by walking daily "in the fear of the LORD." Who is doing that today? Who can define what it really means? Living in the fear of the Lord is not fearing that God will put His hand of retribution *on* you; rather, it is fearing that He might take His hand of blessing and anointing *off* of you. It is no wonder Solomon concluded the book of Ecclesiastes with these words: "Let us hear the conclusion of the whole matter: Fear God and keep His commandments, for this is man's all" (12:13). Now when the wisest man who ever lived said this and was inspired by the Holy Spirit Himself to say it, we should perk up our ears.

Living in the fear of the Lord is the very beginning of the journey toward wisdom.

This wisdom, which we all so desperately need, comes to us by the living Word—by the Lord Jesus Christ Himself, who is "the power of God and the wisdom of God . . . [and] who became for us wisdom from God" (1 Corinthians 1:24, 30). True wisdom begins and ends with Jesus. We come to know this living Word through His written Word, the Bible. This is why Paul, in his last letter before being beheaded, wrote to Timothy, saying, "From childhood you have known the Holy Scriptures, which are able to make you wise" (2 Timothy 3:15).

As we journey through the wisdom of Proverbs and Ecclesiastes, we find Jesus on every page. He is the personification of wisdom, and He freely dispenses it to all those who ask. Go ahead . . . ask!

17 FINDING JESUS IN THE SONG OF SOLOMON

He Is Our Bridegroom

He brought me to the banqueting house, and his banner over me was love. . . . My beloved is mine, and I am his.

—SONG OF SOLOMON 2:4, 16

*T*he song of songs, which is Solomon's" (Song of Solomon 1:1)—with these words, King Solomon launched into a poetic and at times graphic picture of two lovers who become bridegroom and bride. All religious Jews, to this day, read this book every year during their feast of Passover, in the same way they read Esther in the celebration Purim and Ruth during the feast of Pentecost. There are three main characters in this song. Along with Solomon, there is the Shulamite, a rural girl whose beauty caught the king's ever-roving eye. There is also the shepherd who had won the heart of the girl and to whom she remained faithful and true.

The song centers around the love of the shepherd and the young girl; she representing the church, the bride of Christ, you and me, and he representing the Lord Jesus who has won the believer's heart. The story is rich in typology and symbolism on every page. Despite the negative influence of her family, the efforts of Solomon and his harem to win her over, and her virtual imprisonment for a time, the couple remain true to each other through the entire saga. We have no reason to doubt the historical validity of the story, but the real message is embedded in the spiritual lessons that run deep through every verse.

The Song of Solomon has found its place in the canon of sacred Scripture as a picture of the love of Christ, the Bridegroom, for His church, the Bride. This theme is further illustrated in Paul's treatment of the relationship of a husband and wife in the Ephesian epistle (5:25–33). After his detailed listing of the responsibilities of a husband and a wife, Paul zeroed in on the heart of the entire matter when he said, "This is a great mystery, but I speak concerning Christ and the church" (v. 32). Paul did not mean a mystery in the sense of something vague and mysterious; rather, he spoke of a sacred secret, a divine revelation. The church was unknown to those in the Old Testament, and not until we can understand the love of Christ for His church can we grasp the duties of husband and wife.

The mystery of which Paul spoke began back in Eden's garden when God caused a deep sleep to come upon Adam, and his bride was taken out of his side (Genesis 2:21–22). She was bone of his bones and flesh of his flesh. On the cross God caused a deep sleep to come upon the Lord Jesus and out of His wounded side came His bride, the church. This is the "great mystery." He is speaking of Christ and the church. My relationship with my spouse, and your relationship with your spouse, are to be a picture of that. And nowhere in all the Bible is it more beautifully revealed than here in the Song of Solomon.

There is no single, more intimate, more sacred earthly union than the one between a husband and a wife. Yet even that relationship gives us only a glimpse of the deeply intimate relationship between us and our Lord. The Lord Jesus is my Bridegroom. He is the lover of my soul. He is the One who stole my heart. And I am His bride. This means I share His love. Repeatedly in this Song of Solomon, the bride calls her bridegroom her "lover." This is something beautiful they share together. We, as believers, share the love of our Lord for us and our love for Him. It also means that from now on we share His name. That is what a bride does when she is married. She unashamedly takes the name of her husband. Think about it. We are called "Christians" for this very reason.

> The Lord Jesus is my Bridegroom. He is the lover of my soul.

This love story ends with the coming of the shepherd (Song of Solomon 8:5–14). They exchange their vows of love to one another forever. As we are reading these words, our hearts are turned to the coming of our Bridegroom, the Lord Jesus. The book ends with a simple request from the bridegroom: "Your voice—let me hear it!" (v. 13). The shepherd's last request is to hear his bride's voice speaking words of love to him and to him alone. How our Lord longs to hear our voice whispering words of love to Him today.

When the resurrected Christ appeared to the Emmaus disciples and "beginning at Moses and all the Prophets, He expounded to them *in all the Scriptures* the things concerning Himself" (Luke 24:27, emphasis added), we don't know specifically those to which He pointed. But I have to wonder if Jesus mentioned this Song of Solomon. I can almost hear Him saying, "It is all about Me . . . and all about you! I am your Bridegroom. I love you with a never-ending love and long to see you return that love to Me. Let Me hear your voice." Go ahead and say it: "I love You, Lord." Read this Song of Solomon again, and you will find Jesus in every verse. He is our Bridegroom.

18 FINDING JESUS IN ISAIAH

He Is the Suffering Servant

He was wounded for our transgressions, He was bruised for our iniquities. . . . All we like sheep have gone astray; we have turned, every one, to his own way; and the LORD has laid on Him the iniquity of us all. . . . He was led as a lamb to the slaughter, and as a sheep before its shearers is silent, so He opened not His mouth.

—ISAIAH 53:5–7

*T*hroughout this journey through the Old Testament, we have been finding Jesus in every book of the Bible. The sun of God's redemptive revelation began to rise and cast shadows way back in Genesis where we found Jesus as the substitutionary sacrifice, the ram at Abraham's altar. The rising sun continued its ascent as we came to Exodus, and there in chapter 12 we found Jesus, our Passover Lamb. The blood of that innocent sacrifice meant for the Israelites what the blood of Christ means for us: freedom from slavery and deliverance from death. When we arrive here at the prophecy of Isaiah, the sun of God's revelation casts a perfect shadow of our coming Messiah, the Lord Jesus. In minute detail, Isaiah 53 describes the excruciating death of our own suffering servant, Jesus.

Isaiah was writing these words seven centuries before the coming of Christ. And yet God pulled back the veil and allowed the prophet Isaiah to see the future sacrifice of the Messiah as though it had already happened. He wrote these prophetic words in past tense—"He *was* wounded. . . . He *was* bruised. . . . He *was* afflicted" (Isaiah 53:5–7, emphasis added). We get the idea that Isaiah was standing there at the cross, along with Mary and John, taking copious notes, an eyewitness to the greatest event in human history. The entire fifty-third chapter of Isaiah is the clearest picture of Christ in the entire Old Testament.

We not only find a poignant and perfect picture of Jesus in this chapter of Scripture, but we also see a very revealing picture of ourselves as well. The prophet said, "All we like sheep have gone astray; we have turned, every one, to his own way" (v. 6). This metaphorical expression is used repeatedly throughout Scripture. The only way to comprehend the deep meaning of this passage is to glean an insight into how we, in fact, do resemble these wooly creatures.

Fact number one: sheep are directionless. They tend to simply wander aimlessly along the hillsides with no sense of direction whatsoever. In much the same way, a lot of us seem to wander through life without any sense of direction, void of any real perceived purpose.

Fact number two: sheep are defenseless. Almost every

other animal has some type of defense mechanism. Rabbits can run. Dogs can bite. Cats can scratch. Bees can sting. Porcupines can puncture. Goats can butt. Skunks . . . well, you get the point. But sheep? They are not prepared for fight or flight. Men and women without Christ are helpless and hopeless against "wiles of the devil" (Ephesians 6:11). They are ill-equipped to fight off or flee from an attack.

> Men and women without Christ are helpless and hopeless against "wiles of the devil" (Ephesians 6:11).

Since we all find ourselves "like sheep," and since "we turned, every one, to his own way," God must come to our rescue. And He has! Thus we read, "And the LORD has laid on Him the iniquity of us all" (Isaiah 53:6). There is no clearer explanation of what transpired on the cross than these words of Isaiah. We learn so much about His death for us in this chapter.

First, it was *voluntary*: "He opened not His mouth" (Isaiah 53:7). Jesus would echo this thought when He said, "I lay down My life. . . . No one takes it from Me, but I lay it down of Myself" (John 10:17–18).

Christ's death was not only voluntary but *vicarious*. "The LORD has laid on Him the iniquity of us all" (Isaiah 53:6). He died in my place. He died in your place. He died our death in the then and there so we could live His life in the here and now. He took our sin so we could take His righteousness.

The death of Christ was also *vital*. It was necessary. The sacrifices of a million bulls and goats could never take away our sin. In fact, Isaiah concluded by saying, "It pleased the LORD to bruise Him" (v. 10). This is a hard saying. God was not taking pleasure in watching the agony, suffering, and death of His only begotten Son. No, a thousand times, no! What pleased the Father was—when the suffering and sacrifice were complete—there was the possibility of a relationship with any and all of us who would come to Him by faith in His Son to receive the free gift of eternal and abundant life.

In the most focused and clear picture in all the Bible, we find Jesus in Isaiah, walking through every verse of this prophecy. He is the Christ . . . our sin-bearer . . . the Son of the living God.

19 FINDING JESUS IN JEREMIAH AND LAMENTATIONS

He Is Our Weeping Prophet

Oh, that my head were waters, and my eyes a fountain of tears, that I might weep day and night for the slain of the daughter of my people!
—JEREMIAH 9:1

*G*od raised up His prophet Jeremiah about forty years before the Babylonians destroyed and plundered the Holy City of Jerusalem. Repeatedly, through tears, Jeremiah pled with his people to repent in order to avoid the coming disaster. His deep lament is recorded in the book we now know as Lamentations, the most sorrowful of all the books of the Bible, written by the most heartbroken of all the Bible writers. It is no wonder Jeremiah bears the nickname "the Weeping Prophet." If we had the original manuscripts of these two books, we would likely find page after page stained with his tears.

Jeremiah was so filled with sadness he lamented, "Even when I cry and shout, He shuts out my prayer. . . . My strength and my hope have perished from the LORD" (Lamentations 3:8, 18). But before he lost all faith, awakened by his remembrance of God's faithfulness, Jeremiah reminded us that "Through the LORD's mercies we are not consumed, because

His compassions fail not. They are new every morning; great is Your faithfulness. 'The LORD is my portion, . . . therefore I hope in Him!'" (vv. 22–24).

Jeremiah was the physical manifestation of the reality of how God felt in having to judge His own people for their sins and rebellion. And so he wept and wept, all through these two books he left for us. It is no wonder that we find Jesus on more than one occasion weeping in the Gospels. Behind the shortest verse in all the Bible, "Jesus wept" (John 11:35), we find Jesus to be our own weeping prophet.

On two of the occasions we find our Lord weeping, He was on the Mount of Olives, which is opposite Jerusalem, the same city over which Jeremiah wept. At the tomb of Lazarus, Jesus wept—though not because Lazarus was dead. In fact, to prepare His disciples for His own resurrection, Jesus raised Lazarus back to life. Instead, Jesus wept because Lazarus's two sisters, Mary and Martha, were heartbroken and weeping. Tears touch the heart of God . . . your tears . . . my tears. Our great God is touched by our broken hearts and weeps with us. Jesus knew that His tears needed no interpreter. They spoke quite clearly of His love and His compassion. We are blessed to serve a Lord who weeps with us over our sorrows, who is touched by our broken hearts.

> Behind the shortest verse in all the Bible, "Jesus wept" (John 11:35), we find Jesus to be our own weeping prophet.

On the western slope of the Mount of Olives, we find Jesus weeping again. This time over our sins, troubled by our blinded eyes. For many, Palm Sunday was about the crowds, the shouts of Hosanna, the parade, the pep rally. But all that was a sham. And our Lord knew it. Within a few days, those same crowds would be gone and those who remained would turn their cheers into jeers. Sitting on the back of a donkey, descending the Mount of Olives among the throngs and the hosannas, we would think He would be smiling and waving to the adoring crowds. But look closer: "Now as He drew near, He saw the city and wept over it" (Luke 19:41). Can you hear Him through His tears? "If you had known, even you, especially in this your day, the things that make for your peace! But now they are hidden from your eyes" (v. 42).

And so our Lord sat on the Mount of Olives that day and wept, pouring out His heart over our sin and neglect. The Lord Jesus is still touched by our broken hearts and troubled by our blinded eyes. The last time tears are mentioned in the Bible is in Revelation 21:4. It reveals the beautiful scene that will unfold in heaven: "God will wipe away every tear from their eyes." This is our hope. King David said it best: "For His anger is but for a moment, His favor is for life; weeping may endure for a night, but joy comes in the morning" (Psalm 30:5).

20 FINDING JESUS IN EZEKIEL

He Is Our Glory

The Spirit lifted me up and brought me into the inner court; and behold, the glory of the LORD filled the temple.

—EZEKIEL 43:5

While God used Jeremiah to warn the people of Jerusalem of their coming destruction, He used Ezekiel to be His prophetic voice during their days of exile in Babylonian captivity. Along with Daniel and Revelation, the book of Ezekiel is filled with visions, dreams, symbolisms, allegories, prophecies, and parables. God spoke through the various visions of Ezekiel to remind His people that even though they were far away from their Holy City, they still were subject to God's laws and statutes. Ezekiel thundered forth message after message of warnings to God's people, but he wrapped each of them in a ribbon of hope.

Ezekiel's recurring and primary theme was in extolling God's glory. He told how God had taken from them their most prized possession, the very thing on which they were so dependent: God's presence among them. The presence of God had been with them since the days of their wilderness wanderings and through the years of worship in the temple where His Shekinah Glory would visit the Holy of Holies. Ezekiel's words tell of how God's glory departed the Holy of Holies (Ezekiel 9:3). From the temple, Ezekiel revealed how the glory of God moved to the famed Eastern Gate (10:19) and, finally, how it hovered over the Mount of Olives to the east (11:23).

Not long after God removed His glory, the temple was destroyed and His glory never returned, *until* . . . on a starlit night in Bethlehem when, as John described it, "The Word was with God, and the Word was God. . . . And the Word became flesh and dwelt among us, and we beheld His glory, the glory as of the only begotten of the Father, full of grace and truth" (John 1:1, 14). And through His death and resurrection and the coming of His Holy Spirit to indwell the believer, Jesus made a way for God's glory to once again abide with His people. Jesus is God's glory abiding in human flesh. His high intercessory prayer on the evening before His crucifixion still resonates today—"Father, I desire that they also whom You gave Me may be with Me where I am, that they may behold My glory which You have given Me; for You loved Me before the foundation of the world" (John 17:24).

Ezekiel concluded his prophecy by describing a day to come when God's redeemed people will worship in a new millennial temple, and then in a building not made with hands, in the New Jerusalem. Until then, God, who once had a temple for His people, now has a people for His temple. You and me. "Do you not know that your body is the temple of the Holy Spirit who is in you, whom you have from God, and you are not your own?" (1 Corinthians 6:19). In the language of the New Testament, there are two distinct Greek words translated into our English word *temple*. One describes the entire Temple Mount, even including the portico of the temple where Jesus drove out the money changers (Mark 11:15). The other describes only the inner sanctuary itself, the Holy of Holies, the holiest of all places where the Shekinah Glory of God filled the room as He visited with His people.

When the Bible speaks of our bodies being the "temple" of the Holy Spirit today, it is this latter word that is used to describe it. This is not just an awesome thought but an awesome reality. You are God's Holy of Holies. You are His place of worship. You are where His glory dwells. Right now. Christ in you. Jesus is the manifestation of the glory of God. No wonder the Scriptures remind us that we "were bought at a price; therefore glorify God in your body and in your spirit, which are God's" (1 Corinthians 6:20).

Throughout the pages of Ezekiel, we find Jesus . . . sometimes in type, sometimes in visions, sometimes in dreams, and always in prophecies. But

> You are God's Holy of Holies. You are His place of worship.

primarily we find Him as God's own glory who today longs to fill our lives as He once filled the Holy of Holies with His abiding presence. We have something the original hearers of Ezekiel's prophecy did not have. We have the promise of Christ's abiding presence always, for He left us with these final words: "I am with you always, even to the end of the age" (Matthew 28:20).

Anyone, and everyone, who has come to Christ for the forgiveness of sins and trusted in His finished work on the cross knows the reality of God's promise given in Ezekiel 11:19–20: "I will give them one heart, and I will put a new spirit within them, and take the stony heart out of their flesh, and give them a heart of flesh, that they may walk in My statutes and keep My judgments and do them; and they shall be My people, and I will be their God." The Christian life is not a changed life. It is an *exchanged* life. Christ takes out our old heart and puts one in us that is brand-new. Yes, we find Jesus in Ezekiel . . . He is the manifestation of God's glory!

21 FINDING JESUS IN DANIEL

He Is the Fourth Man in the Fiery Furnace

Then King Nebuchadnezzar was astonished; and he rose in haste and spoke, saying to his counselors, "Did we not cast three men bound into the midst of the fire?"

They answered and said to the king, "True, O king."

"Look!" he answered, "I see four men loose, walking in the midst of the fire; and they are not hurt, and the form of the fourth is like the Son of God."

—DANIEL 3:24–25

*F*rom time to time, throughout history, there have been those who have stood up for their beliefs in the face of tremendous cultural pressures even at the risk of extreme personal danger. In the third chapter of the book of Daniel, it is Shadrach, Meshach, and Abed-Nego who take center stage. King Nebuchadnezzar made an image of gold and placed it on the Plains of Dura. On the assigned date and time, everyone gathered there and was ordered to bow down and worship the golden image. These three young Hebrews refused and met the horrible fate of being thrown into the midst of a fiery furnace for their insubordination.

The thrilling deliverance from certain death of these three men is a comfort and challenge to each of us in a culture that is more and more intolerant of our Christian faith. Theirs is the story of faith triumphing over fear. It is the story of courage triumphing over cowardice. It is the story of conviction triumphing over compromise. These three men live on in memory today to teach us some valuable life lessons. God, for instance, never promises us that when we take a stand for Him, we will avoid our own fiery furnace experiences in life. He didn't keep these three faithful followers from that trying experience; instead, He did something better. He got in there with them, loosed their bonds, and delivered them . . . and He will do the same for you and me.

> God . . . never promises us that when we take a stand for Him, we will avoid our own fiery furnace experiences in life.

When confronted by the king about their failure to bow to the image, Shadrach, Meshach, and Abed-Nego had an immediate reply ready. They didn't have to think about their options. Their response to the king's inquiry as to the truth of their failure to bow to his image revealed an amazing perspective:

"Shadrach, Meshach, and Abed-Nego answered and said to the king, . . . 'Our God whom we serve is able to deliver us from the burning fiery furnace, and He will deliver us from your hand, O king. But if not, let it be known to you, O king, that we do not serve your gods, nor will we worship the gold image which you have set up'" (Daniel 3:16–18).

God's ability to deliver them was never in question. They were convinced that He was "able to deliver." The real secret of their positive perspective is found in three little words recorded for all posterity in Daniel 3:18: "*but if not.*" Their faith was in God alone and not in whether He delivered them or not. Some today seem to think that if they are delivered from a fiery furnace experience then everyone should join in the celebration. *But if not* . . . if they are not delivered, they should quietly find a place to hide so as not to damage God's reputation. Let us not forget that the same God who gave so much to Job also took so much from him. The same God who miraculously delivered Simon Peter from prison allowed James to be killed by Herod's sword in the same chapter of Acts. Interestingly, the three Hebrews, when faced with a life-threatening situation, never asked God to deliver them. They simply threw themselves upon Him and His sovereign will for their lives.

As the story continues, we find our friends in a hot spot, "cast into the midst of the burning fiery furnace" (v. 21). They were standing on the promise God gave us through Isaiah: "When you walk through the fire, you shall not be burned, nor shall the flame scorch you" (Isaiah 43:2). God certainly could have delivered Shadrach, Meshach, and Abed-Nego from the furnace, but He had a better plan. Deliverance *from* the furnace experiences of life is not nearly as significant as deliverance *in* the fiery furnace. God delivered them without a hair of their heads singed and caused the king himself to declare, "Blessed be the God of Shadrach, Meshach, and Abed-Nego, who sent His Angel and delivered His servants who trusted in Him" (Daniel 3:28).

These three young men would not bow in the face of compromise, and they would not bend in the face of cowardice. Consequently, they would not burn in the furnace. The king came to look into the furnace and was astonished. "Look! . . . I see four men loose, walking in the midst of the fire; and they are not hurt, and the form of the fourth is like the Son of God" (v. 25). This statement calls for a brief math lesson. How many went into the fiery furnace? Three. How many did the king see when he peered in? Four. How many came out of the furnace? Three. What does this tell us? Our Lord Jesus is always with us. When we find ourselves in our own furnace experiences of life, if we look close enough, we will find Jesus walking in the flames with us.

We find Jesus right here in the book of Daniel. He is the fourth man in the midst of the burning fiery furnace. Yes, God is in control. He is still able to deliver us. His finger is on the thermostat. He will never leave us or forsake us.

22   FINDING JESUS IN HOSEA

He Is the Dew to His People

"I will be like the dew to Israel."

—HOSEA 14:5

*H*osea 14:5 offers one of the most remarkable and revealing promises in all of Scripture. God promises that He will be like the "dew" to His people. When we arise in the early morning hours and witness the dew covering our front lawn, it should be a reminder of this precious promise. Where does dew come from? Does dew fall? Or does dew rise? Before you are too quick to reply, the answer is neither. Dew just appears when certain conditions are right. We have a word for that—*condensation*. And so it is with our Lord who is just "like the dew" to His people. We pray, "Lord, fall on us." Or "Lord, rise up to meet us." But no. The Lord appears to us in power when certain conditions are right in our own lives.

In this one-sentence object lesson of the dew, Hosea teaches us the power of forgiveness. In fact, Hosea's whole message deals with the importance of forgiving those who have wronged us. Israel had behaved like a prostitute by turning away from the Lord and following after other false and pagan gods (Hosea 1:2). God used Hosea and his wife, Gomer, to illustrate the truth of His own relationship with His chosen people. She was repeatedly unfaithful to Hosea with one illicit and sordid affair after another. She finally sunk so low in her rebellion and in her social standing within the community that she was sold as a slave. In God's desire to illustrate His forgiving love to His own people—even when they had willfully been unfaithful—He instructed Hosea to pursue his wife with the same unfailing and forgiving love, even though she was an adulteress. So Hosea ventured into the slave market and bought Gomer back as his very own. Instead of pointed fingers of accusations or extended rants of "How could you have done this?" Hosea quietly clothed her and took her home, intent to show her love and forgiveness and to woo her heart back to his own.

Just as Hosea purchased Gomer out of the marketplace for his own, so Christ stepped into the marketplace where we were slaves to our own sin. We, too, had played the harlot by turning our backs on the One who loves us like no one else ever has or will. The price He paid to free us from our own slavery was not in silver or gold, yet it was the most valuable purchase price ever paid for anyone or anything: His own life's blood. Peter framed it perfectly: "If you call on the Father, who without partiality judges according to each one's work, conduct yourselves throughout the time of your stay here in fear; knowing that you were not redeemed with corruptible things, like silver or gold, from your aimless conduct received by tradition from your fathers, but with the precious blood of Christ, as of a lamb without blemish and without spot" (1 Peter 1:17–19). He took you and me, clothed our naked bodies with His own righteousness, and one day will robe us in a gown of spotless white and present us faultless before His Father's throne.

Hosea's story is the story of the awesome power of forgiveness. Forgiving others has a liberating effect on us and does far more for our own well-being than it does for the one we forgive. Many of us regularly pray what has become commonly known as "The Lord's Prayer." We pray it aloud corporately in public worship. We whisper its words in times of anxiety or fear. But do we really mean it when we pray, "Forgive us as we forgive others"? Too many of us who have been wronged are saying, "I will forgive her, but I am not going to have anything else to do with her." Or we are saying, "I will forgive him, but I will never forget." Is that really the way we want God to forgive us when we pray this model prayer? Jesus was very plain when addressing the need of His followers to unleash the power of forgiveness. On a green grassy hillside in Galilee, He said, "If you forgive men

> Do we really mean it when we pray, "Forgive us as we forgive others"?

their trespasses, your heavenly Father will also forgive you. But if you do not forgive men their trespasses, neither will your Father forgive your trespasses" (Matthew 6:14–15). And what our Lord preached on that hill in Galilee, He practiced on a hill called Golgotha. As the spikes were being driven into His feet and hands fastening Him to the cross, His repeated prayer was, "Father, forgive them, for they do not know what they do" (Luke 23:34).

Hosea's message to each of us is that there is liberating power in the act of forgiveness. Some of us wonder why we live outside the blessing and provision of God. Could it be there is someone, somewhere, we need to forgive? And when we do, the Lord will become like the "dew" to us. We will not need to pray, "Oh, Lord, fall on me." Nor will we need to pray, "Oh, Lord, rise up to meet and bless me." When certain conditions are right in our own lives—like the forgiving of others—He will just show up like the dew. Here in the middle of this ancient prophecy known as Hosea, we find Jesus. And He is still to this very day "like the dew."

23 FINDING JESUS IN JOEL

He Is the One Who Baptizes
Us in the Holy Spirit

"And it shall come to pass afterward that I will pour out My Spirit
on all flesh; your sons and your daughters shall prophesy, your old
men shall dream dreams, your young men shall see visions. And also
on My menservants and My maidservants I will pour out My Spirit
in those days. . . . And it shall come to pass that whoever calls on the
name of the LORD shall be saved."

—JOEL 2:28–29, 32

n the day of Pentecost, Peter stood before the people on the Temple Mount and declared that this prophecy given by Joel more than eight hundred years earlier was coming to pass before their very eyes. God poured out His Spirit, accompanied by amazing manifestations, just as Joel had foretold. Peter declared, "Let all the house of Israel know assuredly that God has made this Jesus, whom you crucified, both Lord and Christ" (Acts 2:36). Hear him state definitively, "This is what was spoken by the prophet Joel" (v. 16). Peter left no doubt that to call on the name of the Lord, as Joel prophesied, was to call on the name of Jesus.

On the day of Pentecost, all the followers of Christ were

"all with one accord in one place" (v. 1), they were "all filled with the Holy Spirit" (v. 4), and they "were all baptized into one body" (1 Corinthians 12:13). The church, the body of Christ, was born. Pentecost, with the coming of the Holy Spirit to indwell the believer, like Bethlehem, was a one-time event and never needs repeating. It was like Calvary, which was also a one-time event that need never be repeated. At Bethlehem, we see God *with* us. At Calvary, we see God *for* us. At Pentecost, we see God *in* us.

What Joel prophesied and what the early believers experienced was not a baptism *of* the Holy Spirit but a baptism *by* the Holy Spirit into the body of Christ: "For by one Spirit we were all baptized into one body" (1 Corinthians 12:13). The Holy Spirit is the Baptizer who, upon our conversion, immerses us into the body of Christ. For thirty-three years the world looked upon the physical body of Christ. With His feet He walked among us, sometimes among great throngs of people, other times in the solitude of a single searching soul. From His lips emerged the most tender and penetrating words ever spoken. Through His piercing eyes He looked deep into the hidden recesses of hearts. Through His ears He listened patiently to pleas for mercy. Through His hands He touched at the point of greatest need.

Today, you and I are the visible "body of Christ" being watched by a seeking world so desperately in need of His touch.

We each occupy a special place in His body. Like our own bodies, when one member suffers it affects the whole body. You are vitally important to God, and His body will never be complete without you serving in that part of the body to which you are assigned. There is something for you to do in the body of Christ that no one else can do quite like you can.

The truth is often stated that the church was a mystery, a hidden secret unrevealed to the Old Testament writers and saints. But for a moment, God drew back the curtain and let Joel see what was to come. And Joel took pen in hand and wrote it down. There was coming a day that would usher in the "last days" when God would pour out His Spirit on all flesh. From that day forward, until Christ's glorious Second Coming, the Spirit would baptize each believer into the body of Christ. And the result? In Joel's own words, "And it shall come to pass that whoever calls on the name of the LORD shall be saved" (Joel 2:32). And true to his word, it has come to pass! In one of the most often quoted verses in the New Testament, the apostle Paul would borrow these words from Joel when writing to the believers in Rome, and to us, saying, "For 'whoever calls on the name of the LORD shall be saved'" (Romans 10:13).

We find Jesus here in the book of Joel. He is the One who baptizes us in the Holy Spirit. And these ancient words are still true . . . "Whoever calls on the name of the LORD shall be saved."

24 FINDING JESUS IN AMOS

He Is Our Plumb Line

Thus He showed me: Behold, the Lord stood on a wall made with a plumb line, with a plumb line in His hand. And the Lord said to me, "Amos, what do you see?" And I said, "A plumb line." Then the Lord said: "Behold, I am setting a plumb line in the midst of My people Israel."

—AMOS 7:7–8

The prophet Amos used the vivid imagery of a plumb line to warn the people of the northern kingdom of Israel that God has a righteous standard by which He will judge His people. A plumb line is a string with a weight attached to one end. When the string is held in such a way that the weight dangles freely, it eventually comes to a halt so that an exact vertical line can be accomplished. Carpenters still use plumb lines today to keep their work exactly straight and in line. In essence, the plumb line applies God's exact law of gravity to find right angles. A plumb line never changes or moves with the wishes or whims of the carpenter. It remains true always, and all work must line up with it or risk being crooked and out of line.

Jesus, God's true plumb line, came down from heaven

into our very midst. He did not just set a standard by meeting all the righteous demands of God's laws; He *is* the standard! He *is* our plumb line. He clothed Himself in human flesh and lived a perfect life uncontaminated by the world's sin. He met all the righteous demands of the law. And the truth is, not one of us measures up. We are all "off center." Unlike Him, we have all sinned and come short (Romans 3:23) of God's demands of righteousness. God holds His plumb line up beside our lives and asks, "How do you measure up?" He cannot and will not ignore our sin.

The psalmist asked a probing and penetrating question: "Who may ascend into the hill of the LORD? Or who may stand in His holy place?" (Psalm 24:3). And no sooner did he ask the question than he provided the answer: "He who has clean hands and a pure heart" (v. 4). This is God's plumb line: our actions ("clean hands") and our attitudes ("pure hearts"). And not a single one of us meets this standard—not on our own. Our hands are dirty with sin, and our hearts are far from pure. In fact, the Bible reminds us that "the heart is deceitful above all things, and desperately wicked" (Jeremiah 17:9).

The hill described in Psalm 24 is Mount Calvary. Only one person in all of human history met the righteous demands of the law accompanied by the two qualifications—the plumb line—of clean hands and a pure heart: the Lord Jesus Christ.

His hands were clean, uncontaminated by sin. His heart was pure. Knowing I was without hope, He descended from heaven to make a way for me to one day ascend to Him there. His clean hands became dirty with my sin and yours. Why? So our dirty hands could become clean. Jesus' pure heart became filled with our sin. Why? So that our sinful hearts could become pure in God's eyes. So, who now shall ascend into the hill of the Lord? You can. I can. If we open the gates of our hearts and let the King of Glory come in.

Like Amos's plumb line, the Lord Jesus came down and by His life set the standard of holiness for us. And since none of us can meet that standard, we must run to Jesus, put our trust in Him, and claim Him as our substitute. Christ alone is our plumb line. It is no wonder the Bible says, "For He made Him who knew no sin to be sin for us, that we might become the righteousness of God in Him" (2 Corinthians 5:21).

> Like Amos's plumb line, the Lord Jesus came down and by His life set the standard of holiness for us.

Into our moral failures and shortcomings, Christ comes to show us God's plumb line, not weighted by the law but weighted by grace. He says to us today, "I am the plumb line. I alone measured up to its perfect standard. But by grace, through faith in Me alone, you can stand in My own righteousness so that when

God tests you with His plumb line, instead of condemning you, He will receive you faultless before His throne."

God is asking you and me what He asked Amos of old: "What do you see?" Do you see it? The cross of Christ has become God's plumb line by which He will judge the world. We find Jesus here in the middle of Amos's ancient prophecy. He is, and ever will be, our standard of righteousness, our plumb line. Run to Him.

25 FINDING JESUS IN OBADIAH

He Is Our Legacy

"But on Mount Zion there shall be deliverance, and there shall be holiness. . . . The house of Jacob shall be a fire . . . but the house of Esau shall be stubble; they shall kindle them and devour them, and no survivor shall remain in the house of Esau," for the LORD has spoken. . . . And the kingdom shall be the LORD's."

—OBADIAH V. 17–18, 21

*Y*our legacy is the lasting influence, whether good or bad, that is left behind after you are gone. Obadiah, the shortest book in the Old Testament, is all about legacy. The enemies to a legacy are obvious in these brief verses—pride and indifference. The fact is, we can never *leave* a legacy until we first *live* a legacy. And no one who ever walked this planet left a more lasting and loving legacy than our Lord Jesus Christ. You and I are a part of a long line of billions of people through the centuries who have been caught up in the flow of His legacy. Obadiah saw into the future and found a legacy springing up from Jacob and through Jesus and His coming kingdom. He closed his brief book with these words: "And the kingdom shall be the LORD's" (Obadiah v. 21).

God has left a legacy for His people. This is the message

of Obadiah: Israel will reclaim its inheritance from Him, and Edom will vanish from the earth like "stubble" that is kindled with fire and devoured. Obadiah is prophesying about the twin brothers, Jacob and Esau, born of Isaac. They came out of the womb fighting with each other and never stopped. Esau was completely disinterested in spiritual matters and gave up his birthright to his brother, Jacob. The ancient Edomites are the descendants of Esau, and Israel came out of the loins of Jacob. Like the twin brothers, Israel and Edom had a long history of rivalry and conflict. God blessed Jacob, and from him would come the legacy of the promised Jewish Messiah, our Lord Jesus Christ. Obadiah's warning to Edom is also to any of us who, like Esau, are indifferent to God's purposes: "Shame shall cover you, and you shall be cut off forever" (Obadiah v. 10). The warning was fulfilled. Search the whole world over, and you will not find an Edomite alive today. But Israel is alive and well, and Messiah Jesus' legacy lives on in everyone who is called by His name.

Calls to leave a lasting legacy wind their way through the pages of the Bible. The psalmist Asaph framed it well: "We have heard and known, and our fathers have told us. We will not hide them from their children, telling to the generation to come the praises of the LORD, and His strength and His wonderful works that He has done" (Psalm 78:3–4). Upon leading the Israelites, the children of Jacob, into the promised land after decades of wilderness wandering, Joshua said, "When your children ask their fathers in time to come, saying, 'What are these stones?' then you shall let your children know, saying, 'Israel crossed over this Jordan on dry land'; for the LORD your God dried up the waters of the Jordan before you until you had crossed over" (Joshua 4:21–23). Joshua left a legacy of the Lord's mighty power. Solomon reminded us that "a good man leaves an inheritance to his children's children" (Proverbs 13:22). In the New Testament, we find Paul speaking about the importance of leaving Christ's legacy with those who come after us. To the Philippians, he said, "The things which you learned and received and heard and saw in me, these do, and the God of peace will be with you" (Philippians 4:9). And in the last letter Paul penned, from a damp, dingy prison cell in Rome, he challenged Timothy, saying, "And the things that you have heard from me among many witnesses, commit these to faithful men who will be able to teach others also" (2 Timothy 2:2). Paul knew that every Christian generation has the responsibility to pass the legacy of Christ to the next.

> Paul knew that every Christian generation has the responsibility to pass the legacy of Christ to the next.

Jesus is here, in Obadiah. He is our legacy. David was speaking of Christ when he said, "Great is the LORD, and greatly to be praised; and His greatness is unsearchable. One generation shall praise Your works to another, and shall declare Your mighty acts" (Psalm 145:3–4). Your legacy is Christ's legacy. Pass it on. Life is short. *Live* a legacy so that you might *leave* a legacy to those who come after you. Make sure that your name is not just carved on a cold tombstone in some isolated cemetery somewhere but carved on the warm hearts of those around you. Join King David in saying, "Great is the LORD, and greatly to be praised." Pass on the legacy of Christ!

26   FINDING JESUS IN JONAH

He Is the God of the Second Chance

Now the word of the LORD came to Jonah the second time, saying, "Arise, go to Nineveh, that great city, and preach to it the message that I will tell you." So Jonah arose and went to Nineveh, according to the word of the LORD.

—JONAH 3:1–3

*T*he pages of history are replete with the heartwarming stories of men and women who have been down and came back to take advantage of the second chance. Abraham Lincoln is a prime example. Defeated for the state legislature in 1832, defeated for Congress in 1843, again in 1848, defeated for the Senate in 1854, then again in 1858, he was elected president of the United States in 1860. In the field of literature, there is John Bunyan who, when thrown into prison, could have easily given up. From his dungeon cell he penned the words of *The Pilgrim's Progress*, which have blessed millions across the generations. We all love a comeback story. Tiger Woods, one of the greatest golfers of all time, after being sidelined for years with recurring back surgeries came back to win the 2019 Masters against all odds. There is something about the human spirit that loves to see people come through when there seems to be no way.

Most of us have heard Jonah's saga from childhood. God instructed him to go to the city of Nineveh and preach. Instead, he boarded a ship headed in the opposite direction, found himself in a violent storm, was cast overboard, and was swallowed by a great fish. For three days and three nights, he tossed in the belly of that monster as it journeyed through the depths of the sea. Then God commanded the fish, and it "vomited Jonah onto dry land" (Jonah 2:10). And "the word of the LORD came to Jonah the second time" (Jonah 3:1). He took advantage of it, got up, and headed straight for Nineveh and the second chance. Second chances in life are not only possible, they can be profitable.

But the ultimate comeback story of all time took place two thousand years ago in the city of Jerusalem. The Lord Jesus Christ was crucified on a Roman cross and placed in a borrowed tomb. He was *dead.* Some of His closest followers, dejected and defeated, even exclaimed, "We were hoping that it was He who was going to redeem Israel" (Luke 24:21). They fled the scene, leaving their hope buried in the tomb. But on the third day Jesus came back. He burst forth from the

> The ultimate comeback story of all time took place two thousand years ago in the city of Jerusalem.

tomb to live forevermore. Earlier, when Jesus predicted His future resurrection, He pointed back in time to the prophet Jonah as if to say, "I was there with Jonah. Those were My words that came to him a second time." Once earlier, when asked for some sign of His authenticity, He replied, "No sign will be given to it except the sign of the prophet Jonah. For as Jonah was three days and three nights in the belly of the great fish, so will the Son of Man be three days and three nights in the heart of the earth" (Matthew 12:39–40). Jonah was *the* sign of our Lord's own death and resurrection. Our Lord was showing us that He was the One greater than Jonah who would "come back" from the grave, the living Lord and Savior, still offering the second chance today. It is never too late for a new beginning with Him.

Standing at the grave of Lazarus, Jesus proclaimed, "I am the resurrection and the life. He who believes in Me, though he may die, he shall live. . . . Do you believe this?" (John 11:25–26). I often wonder where our Lord inflected this question. I think He may have asked it like this—"Do *you*, you and you only, you and no one else, do *you* believe this?" After all, this is life's bottom-line question. Our personal faith is the only acceptable response to the Christian gospel. Jesus was not inquiring about intellectual assent here. It is one thing to know the gospel on an intellectual level. It is one thing to try to conform to a set of moral standards. But life's bottom-line question begs to know if *you* have personally transferred your trust from your own human efforts to Christ and His finished work for your eternal salvation. Do *you* believe this?

If we look deep enough, we can find Jesus in every book of the Bible. He is here in the midst of the book of Jonah. He is that "word of the LORD" that came to Jonah a second time. He is the God of the second chance to any and all who will believe. You can begin your own comeback story today . . . by faith . . . in Him.

27 FINDING JESUS IN MICAH

He Is Our Peace

"But you, Bethlehem Ephrathah, though you are little among the thousands of Judah, yet out of you shall come forth to Me the One to be Ruler in Israel, whose goings forth are from old, from everlasting. . . . He shall be great . . . and this One shall be peace."

—MICAH 5:2, 4–5

This "One," this coming Messiah, who is to be born in Bethlehem would not just be the bearer of peace, but the very source of peace itself. "This One shall be peace" (Micah 5:5). And so as to leave no doubt of His deity, Micah revealed that this coming One's "goings forth are from of old, from everlasting" (v. 2). Though the Messiah was to be born in Bethlehem, this was not the beginning of His existence. He is from everlasting to everlasting. He has always been. He will always be. This promised One was not just a man . . . He was and is God, who stepped over the portals of heaven and clothed Himself in human flesh.

Hundreds of years after Micah penned these words, Magi, wise men from the East, would see His star and follow it over a long journey of hundreds of miles to the holy land. The religious leaders of the time knew all the prophecies of the promised, coming Messiah of Israel and, thus, upon the Magi's inquiry of King Herod, they instructed Herod of Micah's prophecy. This coming "Prince of Peace" (Isaiah 9:6) was to be born in the seemingly insignificant little village of Bethlehem, just south of Jerusalem. In Micah's own words, "little among the thousands of Judah" (5:2).

Through the pen of the prophet Micah, God revealed Bethlehem as the divinely handpicked city that would cradle the Son of God. Think of it. Of all the places for Messiah to be born, why Bethlehem? Why not Jerusalem? It was the seat of religious power. Why not Rome? It was the seat of political power. Why not Athens? It was the seat of intellectual power. Through Micah, God was sending a message. The hope of the world is not in religion, nor is it in politics, nor is it in philosophy. The hope of the world is in a Savior. The Bible calls Him the "Prince of Peace." And this same Jesus, born in Bethlehem, is our source of peace this very day.

By choosing Bethlehem, God was also saying to us that it was a place of potential. He is reminding all of us that, in His economy, the small shall be great, the last shall be first. God saw Bethlehem as a place of limitless potential. And He sees you in the same light . . . not just for who you are, but also for who you could be. You are a person of potential in His eyes.

We live in a troubled world today, desperately in search of peace and yet totally unaware of the biblical truth that there will never be true peace without being centered in the One who is from everlasting to everlasting and who is called the Prince of Peace. People march up and down our streets flashing the peace sign, calling for world peace. But there will never be peace on a global scale without first having peace on a national level. Peace on a national level is impossible without first having peace on a state level. We will never experience peace in our state until we have peace in our counties and in our cities. I live in Dallas, Texas, and I can testify by watching the evening news nightly that we do not have peace in our city. It is impossible to have peace in our city until we have peace in our neighborhoods, and this is futile until we have peace on our street. To carry it further, you cannot have peace on your street until you have peace on your block. And peace on your own block is impossible without peace in your home. Finally, peace in your home is impossible unless *you* have peace in your own heart. The bottom line? You will never have peace in your heart until the Prince of Peace Himself, the Lord Jesus, comes to live in you by faith. There is no true and lasting peace without Him!

We find Jesus here in Micah. He is our peace. And on the night before He was crucified on a Roman cross outside the city walls of Jerusalem, this One who was born in Bethlehem left us these parting words: "Peace I leave with you, My peace I give to you; not as the world gives do I give to you. Let not your heart be troubled, neither let it be afraid" (John 14:27). Yes, "this One shall be peace" (Micah 5:5).

28 FINDING JESUS IN NAHUM

He Is Our Stronghold in the Day of Trouble

The LORD is good, a stronghold in the day of trouble; and He knows those who trust in Him.

—NAHUM 1:7

*N*ahum is the prophet who prophesied the fall of Nineveh, the Assyrian capital. But in the midst of the doom and gloom of his book, there arises a reminder that God is a good God and He knows those who are His. In fact, Nahum revealed Jesus is a "stronghold," a safe haven into which you and I may run in our own day of trouble. King Solomon earlier echoed these words, saying, "The name of the LORD is a strong tower; the righteous run to it and are safe" (Proverbs 18:10).

In biblical times kings built fortresses, called "strongholds," where, if necessary, they could retreat and be able to defend themselves and stave off enemies. One of the great builders of history was the first-century Judean king, Herod the Great. To this day, his protective stronghold, the Herodian, can be visited in the Judean hills south of Bethlehem. But his most magnificent accomplishment was Masada down in the Jordan

Valley near the Dead Sea. Located high atop a tall mountain, he built a three-tiered palace on the cliffs of its northern edge. This entire fortress was completely self-sustaining, consisting of large water cisterns, aqueducts, agricultural areas, storage rooms, Roman baths, and even a synagogue.

Masada, a popular tourist attraction today in Israel, is best known for what took place there almost two thousand years ago. When Titus and his Roman legions besieged the city of Jerusalem in AD 70, a small band of nine hundred Jewish zealots escaped the burning city and fled to the stronghold of Masada. Upon hearing this, the Roman army made its way there and encircled the mountain stronghold. To this very day, the remnants of their camps can be seen around the base of this huge mountain. The Jews held out on top of the fortress of Masada for three years. It was their stronghold in their time of trouble.

Where do you flee when you need refuge? In the days of King David, we find him time and again fleeing to one of his strongholds, saying, "The LORD is a stronghold for the oppressed, a stronghold in times of trouble. And those who know your name put their trust in you, for you, O LORD, have not forsaken those who seek you" (Psalm 9:9–10 ESV). He added, "The LORD is my light and my salvation; whom shall I fear? The LORD is the stronghold of my life; of whom shall I be afraid?" (Psalm 27:1 ESV).

We, too, have a stronghold when trouble comes. The Lord is our Stronghold. We can take refuge in Him. The night before the crucifixion, Jesus said, "At that day you will know that I am in My Father, and you in Me, and I in you" (John 14:20). Your stronghold is not in what you are, or who you are, or why you are, but *where* you are.

Jesus told us that He is positioned "in My Father." Then, in the next breath, He revealed that "you [are] in Me." Stop just a moment and think about that. He is your stronghold, and you are "in Him," which is a very safe place to be. If you are *in* Christ and He is *in* the Father, then nothing can get to you that doesn't first have to pass through God the Father and God the Son to reach you. And if it penetrates that fortress, you can rest in the fact that there is a purpose for it to be in your life.

But that is not all. Jesus continued, "And I [am] in you." Can you see it? Christ is taking care of the outside of you (you are in Him), and He is also taking care of the inside of you (He is in you). What better place to find your refuge?

We find Jesus here in the midst of this rather obscure prophecy in the Old Testament. Nahum described Him as your "stronghold," your place of refuge and safety "in the day of trouble." We are left with three important reminders in Nahum 1:7:

> The Lord is our Stronghold. We can take refuge in Him.

First, "the LORD is good." He is a good God and desires to bless us. Second, "He knows those who trust in Him." He knows you *and* loves you. And lastly, He is "a stronghold in the day of trouble." He is right here in the middle of Nahum's book. He is waiting for you to run to Him! And, as He promised, He will never leave you or forsake you.

29 FINDING JESUS IN HABAKKUK

He Is the Personification of Our Hope

Though the fig tree may not blossom, nor fruit be on the vines; though the labor of the olive may fail, and the fields yield no food; though the flock may be cut off from the fold, and there be no herd in the stalls—yet, I will rejoice in the LORD, I will joy in the God of my salvation. The LORD God is my strength; He will make my feet like deer's feet, and He will make me walk on my high hills.

—HABAKKUK 3:17–19

*H*abakkuk lived with a "burden" (Habakkuk 1:1) in a day when hope was almost gone. His prophecy begins with a heartfelt and honest question, "O LORD, how long shall I cry, and You will not hear?" (v. 2). How could a holy God—who had called Israel, His own chosen people, the "apple of His eye" (Deuteronomy 32:10)— now allow the pagan Babylonians to brutally massacre masses of Jews, besiege and ultimately destroy the city of Jerusalem, and carry the brightest Jewish minds back to Babylonian captivity? If we are honest, most of us have asked a similar question when we were living in a moment when it seemed that hope was gone. Habakkuk revealed four realities for anyone and everyone who is in desperate need of hope.

In Habakkuk, chapter 1, we see that hope subsides when we focus all our attention on our problem. Listen to him: "How long shall I cry, and You will not hear? . . . And You will not save. . . . The law is powerless, and justice never goes forth" (Habakkuk 1:2, 4). He was asking what many ask today when faced with a crisis situation: "Where are You, God? Why don't You do something?" Hope has its own way of slipping quietly away when we focus all of our attention on our problem. Like Habakkuk, it leads us to ask a multitude of questions that have no real, satisfactory answers.

But the prophet lifted up his eyes in chapter 2 to reveal to us that hope clings to God's promises. God reminded him that His vision was "yet for an appointed time. . . . Though it tarries, wait for it; because it will surely come" (vv. 2–3). What a timely and comforting promise: "It will surely come." Our hope can rest on the truth that what God promises He will surely perform. In the kingdom of God, we live by promises, not explanations. Naaman almost missed his cure because he was looking for an explanation when God gave him a promise that if he would submerge himself seven times in the Jordan River his leprosy would be cleansed (2 Kings

> In the kingdom of God, we live by promises, not explanations.

5:14). There will be times in life when all we have are the promises of God. But that is enough. Hope comes when we cling to God's promise.

But there is more. Hope realizes that God is in total control. Habakkuk stated, "The LORD is in His holy temple. Let all the earth keep silence before Him" (v. 20). Hope sees that God has not abdicated His throne. He is still in control. Evil may appear to triumph—for a while—but it will not last. God still reigns over the affairs of men, and hope puts its faith in this time-honored truth.

Finally, Christ, our hope, can see past tomorrow. Habakkuk concluded his brief book with an amazing confession: "Though the fig tree may not blossom, nor fruit be on the vines; . . . the olive may fail, and the fields yield no food; . . . no herd in the stalls—*yet* I will rejoice in the LORD, I will joy in the God of my salvation. . . . He will make my feet like deer's feet, and He will make me walk on my high hills" (Habakkuk 3:17–19, emphasis added). This is the same man who began his brief book by shaking his fist in the face of God—his hope almost gone. Now he had found hope in the Lord and could see past tomorrow. He could say the two "I wills" in verse 18 ("I will rejoice . . . I will joy") because of the two "He wills" in verse 19 ("He will make my feet like deer's feet . . . He will make me walk on high hills"). He will enable me like the deer to gracefully scale over any and all obstacles that come my way. And He will lead me on to higher ground. Hope lives in the lives of each of us when we realize the truth of a little phrase that is so often repeated throughout the Bible: "And it came to pass." Whatever it may be that tries to take away your hope will not last; it will come to pass.

Hope is the deep and dire need of so many in today's world. And Jesus Christ is the personification of hope—our only *real* hope. We find Him here walking through these pages in the prophecy of Habakkuk. He is the One, our hope, who enables us to cling to God's promises, to realize that He is still in control, and He is the One who helps us see past all our troubles to a better and a brighter day. Jesus is our hope . . . our only real and lasting hope.

30 FINDING JESUS IN ZEPHANIAH:

He Is the Lord, Mighty to Save

The LORD your God in your midst, the Mighty One, will save; He will rejoice over you with gladness, He will quiet you with His love, He will rejoice over you with singing.

—ZEPHANIAH 3:17

ephaniah was blessed to live in a day when God had visited His people in Judah with genuine revival under the reign of good King Josiah. His word was one of hope and encouragement, pointing to the Lord who was mighty to save, resulting in much rejoicing and singing. Zephaniah helped the people look forward to the day when God would send His own Son "that the world through Him might be saved" (John 3:17).

There is one chapter of the Bible that is consumed with the fruition of this prophecy of Zephaniah who pointed to the One who was mighty to save and who would rejoice over us with singing. Jesus was the master storyteller, and in Luke 15, He told three stories. First, He told the story of the shepherd who searched for and found his lost sheep and then exclaimed, "Rejoice with me, for I have found my sheep which was lost" (Luke 15:6). Next, He told the story of the woman who lost a valuable coin and upon finding it called to her friends and neighbors, saying, "Rejoice with me, for I have found the piece which I lost" (v. 9). But the best known of all our Lord's parables is the story commonly referred to as the prodigal son. When the boy who strayed away came home, the father said to the self-righteous older brother, "It was right that we should make merry and be glad, for your brother was dead and is alive again, and was lost and is found" (v. 32).

This old and often-repeated story of the prodigal son may well be the most misunderstood of all the parables of Jesus. Most every time we hear a sermon or read a devotional from this passage, the wayward son is on center stage. He is the center of attention. The boy took his inheritance, left home, and headed for the bright lights of the big city. There he threw it all away on wine, women, and song. After an extensive job search, he finally ended up feeding swine in a pig pen. When you think about it, that was not a very good place for a Jewish boy to be. But, at last, he "came to himself" (v. 17) and headed home to seek his father's forgiveness. The father saw him coming when he was a long way down the road. The boy came walking, but the father went running to meet him with open arms. No clinched fists, no pointed fingers of accusation, just open arms—wide, loving, forgiving open arms. And, to echo Zephaniah, the father rejoiced over him with gladness, quieted him with his love, and threw a party rejoicing over him with singing.

But don't miss Zephaniah's and Jesus' point. It was the *father* who really had center stage in Jesus' story, not the son. Look at Luke 15:11. Jesus said, "A certain man had two sons." Who is the subject of that sentence? Not either of the sons. The subject of the sentence and the center of the entire story is the father. Jesus told this story to emphasize the father's faithfulness—and His Father's faithfulness. This story is all about showing us the Lord's never-ending love for each and every one of us. It reveals to us the Lord's heart as He rejoices "over one sinner who repents" (v. 10).

In Zephaniah, Jesus is the Lord who is mighty to save. And the moment we come home to Him in true repentance, like the prodigal son, He forgives and forgets. Yes, He is able to "save to the uttermost those who come to God through Him" (Hebrews 7:25). Repentance is a change of mind, which affects a change in volition, which results in a change of action. First, the prodigal changed his mind: "He came to himself" (Luke 15:17). This changed his volition. Hear him say, "I *will* arise and go to my father" (v. 18, emphasis added). Then we

> Repentance is a change of mind, which affects a change in volition, which results in a change of action.

read, "He arose and came to his father" (v. 20). And then the rejoicing began! Jesus is mighty to save!

The real message of this story is that Jesus, at every turn, is continually surprising us with His grace and mercy. We may come walking back to Him, but He will come running to us. Just as Zephaniah's words reveal, He is a merciful, loving, forgiving Savior. We find Jesus right here in Zephaniah. He is the Lord, mighty to save.

31   FINDING JESUS IN HAGGAI

He Is the Restorer of Our Lost Heritage

Thus speaks the LORD of hosts, saying: "This people says, 'The time has not come, the time that the LORD's house should be built.'"

Then the word of the LORD came by Haggai the prophet, saying, "Is it time for you yourselves to dwell in your paneled houses, and this temple to lie in ruins?" Now therefore, thus says the LORD of hosts, "Consider your ways!" . . . Then Haggai, the LORD's messenger, spoke the LORD's message to the people, saying, "I am with you, says the LORD." . . . And they came and worked on the house of the LORD of hosts, their God.

—HAGGAI 1:2–5, 13–14

Haggai's prophetic words come after the return of the Jews to Jerusalem from Babylonian captivity. While Ezra chronicled the remnant on their way back to Jerusalem, Haggai gave us tremendous insight into what happened after they had settled back into their lives in the Holy City. The people had returned with instructions to rebuild the temple, the house of God. They made a good start and laid a solid foundation. But after a while, they went back to their livelihoods, focusing on the building of their own luxurious houses while God's house remained in ruins.

The temple, whose splendor had once been the object of their pride, remained a heap of rubbish and ashes overgrown with weeds. Haggai's passion and prophecies awakened the Jews from their lethargy and inspired them to resume and complete the work of the temple. Continually he spoke of Jesus, not by His name, but by the name of the "Lord of hosts" whose own words moved the people to restore their lost heritage.

The temple was God's dwelling place on earth. His house. It was where He came annually to visit His people on the Day of Atonement, restoring their fractured fellowship with Him. In His great and awesome mercy, God was determined to live among His people as He had in the past. His heart's desire was to restore their lost heritage.

> In His great and awesome mercy, God was determined to live among His people as He had in the past.

We once lived in unbroken fellowship with Him. But we lost that heritage in Eden's garden when we chose to sin and were expelled from paradise (Genesis 3). We have been trying to get back there ever since. The rest of the Bible is the story of God reaching out to us to restore our lost heritage. These ancient words of Haggai call upon us to consider our ways (Haggai 1:5) and listen to His voice as He says to us what He said to the people of Haggai's day, "I am with you" (v. 13).

Hundreds of years after these words of Haggai, Jesus came. He lived a perfect life. He went about doing good, speaking the greatest words ever spoken, and practicing every syllable He preached. Surely His people must have loved Him. But not really. We didn't want Him disrupting our lifestyle, so we crucified Him. He was buried in a borrowed grave. He rose to life three days later and appeared to hundreds in His resurrected body. Then He ascended back to heaven with these parting words, the same precious promise He had given through Haggai—"I am with you always, even to the end of the age" (Matthew 28:20). Jesus is the restorer of our own lost heritage.

In Christ, the presence of God visited our world a final time, not in a temple made and rebuilt with human hands, but in a body that was prepared for Him. Because of His grace we need not enter a temple made of brick and mortar, much less overlaid in gold. God clothed Himself in human flesh; He entered a temple of flesh and blood to meet with us. Fellowship has been restored through Christ. The resounding promise of Haggai, "I am with you," is fulfilled in the lives of all believers today, accompanied by a beautiful addendum: not only is He with us, "He Himself has said, 'I will never leave you nor forsake you'" (Hebrews 13:5).

We find Jesus here in the ancient prophecy of Haggai. He was and always will be the restorer of our lost heritage.

32 FINDING JESUS IN ZECHARIAH

He Is Our Coming Victor

"Rejoice greatly, O daughter of Zion! Shout, O daughter of Jerusalem! Behold, your King is coming to you; He is just and having salvation, lowly and riding on a donkey."

—ZECHARIAH 9:9

echariah lived and prophesied during the days of the post-Babylonian exile. He encouraged the people to complete the rebuilding of Jerusalem and stood head and shoulders above all his minor prophet peers in pointing to Jesus with his messianic predictions and prophecies. Israel was without a king and greatly in need of a leader. In ancient days, kings would ride into the cities they ruled in great pomp and splendor on the back of a stunning white stallion. But Zechariah foretold that Israel's coming Messiah-King would enter Jerusalem in pomp and splendor, not on the back of a stallion, but riding a lowly donkey. He would come not to conquer and control but to bring freedom and peace to the human heart.

And so, the Messiah came, just as promised in "the fullness of the time" (Galatians 4:4), to a Jerusalem that was controlled and ruled by the cruel iron fist of the Roman Empire. The Jews were desperate for a political-military king who would free them from their oppressive occupiers. They knew well the writings and prophecies of Zechariah. But they did not recognize their King when He came, even though Jesus quoted the words of Zechariah 9:9 when He entered the city in triumph (Matthew 21:4–5).

Great crowds had lined the parade route down the Palm Sunday road from the summit of the Mount of Olives, down the western slope, through the Kidron Valley, up the eastern slope of Mount Moriah, and into the gate of the city. There was dancing in the street. The crowds were singing at the top of their lungs as they waved their palm branches. A festive mood permeated the atmosphere. Everyone loves a parade.

But it was all a facade. And Jesus knew it. In a matter of days all those cheers would turn to jeers. Can you picture the Lord Jesus, fulfilling Zechariah's prophecy, riding on a donkey? He is the center of attention. He must have had a smile on His face as He came riding down the mountain, as if He were sitting in a convertible in a parade. The party was on. The people were waving their palm branches, singing and shouting. And then we read these words: "As He drew near, He saw the city and wept over it" (Luke 19:41). Look at Him. In the midst of all the hype and hoopla, He wept.

Tears welled in His eyes, spilled over onto His cheeks, and ran down into His beard.

His kingdom was not of this world. More than eighty times in the Gospels they had heard Him speak of the "kingdom of God." But they didn't get it. They were not celebrating Him; they were celebrating what they thought they might get from Him. Somehow they had read right past the words Zechariah had left them describing this event. They missed it . . . and He knew it. And so our Lord wept.

Those Palm Sunday crowds thought they were getting what they wanted. They thought they were welcoming a king who would deliver them from the oppression of Roman occupation. A few days later, they realized they were not getting what they wanted. So they made Him a king, all right. They made a crown of thorns and pressed it onto His brow. Then, mockingly, they bowed before Him with sarcastic hails to the king. They laughed, they spat in His face, and they beat Him. Then they stripped Him of His clothing and nailed Him to a cross. He was a king—the King. But His kingdom was not of this world; it was a kingdom of the heart.

> He was a king—the King. But His kingdom was not of this world; it was a kingdom of the heart.

True to Zechariah's prophecy, the crowds were rejoicing and shouting, but for all the wrong reasons. What they wanted was not what they needed most.

Jesus had come to free them from the bondage that sin brings to the human heart. And, like some of us, they missed it. Jesus is still passing by our hearts today. He is still saying to us, "If you had known, even you, especially in this your day, the things that make for your peace!" (Luke 19:42). It just might be that the something you think you need right now is not "something" but "Someone."

The day is still coming when our Lord will, indeed, enter Jerusalem, before the eyes of the entire world, riding on the back of a white stallion (Revelation 19:11). On this visit, He will be our conquering King, riding in all His majesty into the Holy City to set up His kingdom of peace. In the words of Zechariah, the prophet, "And the LORD shall be King over all the earth. In that day it shall be—'The LORD is one,' and His name one" (Zechariah 14:9).

Jesus is here in every book of your Bible. He is walking through these pages sometimes in shadow, sometimes in type, and sometimes, as here in Zechariah, in prophecy. What God has promised, He will perform. Make sure you do not miss it!

33 FINDING JESUS IN MALACHI

*He Is the Sun of Righteousness
with Healing in His Wings*

*"But to you who fear My name the Sun of Righteousness shall arise
with healing in His wings."*

—MALACHI 4:2

Malachi, whose name means "messenger of Yahweh," was the last of the Old Testament voices who spoke for God and from God. He is basically unknown, and his final recorded words—"Behold, I will send you Elijah the prophet before the coming of the great and dreadful day of the LORD. And he will turn the hearts of the fathers to the children, and the hearts of the children to their fathers, lest I come and strike the earth with a curse" (Malachi 4:5–6)— usher in a four-hundred-year period when God's voice was silent, until we come to Matthew 1:1 and read "the book of the genealogy of Jesus Christ."

Malachi boldly confronted the failure of the priests of Judah to fear the Lord. Thus he introduced the coming "Sun of Righteousness . . . with healing in His wings" with this caveat—the promise is for those who "fear My name" (Malachi 4:2). Perhaps no Christian discipline in our day is as forgotten as this idea of "living in the fear of the Lord." Who is doing this? Who of us could define what it even means?

Earlier Isaiah asked a probing question, "Who among you fears the LORD?" (Isaiah 50:10). This question is as relevant today as it was 2,500 years ago. This theme, walking in the fear of the Lord, is like a thread woven through the lives of those men and woman in the Bible who were greatly used by God. Noah, "moved with godly fear" (Hebrews 11:7), built the ark. The Proverbs 31 woman was blessed because she "fears the LORD" (v. 30). The young Virgin Mary praised God whose "mercy is on those who fear Him" (Luke 1:50). In Luke 5, Jesus heals a paralytic, and we read that "they were all amazed . . . and were filled with fear" (v. 26). In Acts, the concept of living in the fear of the Lord is on almost every page. After Peter's Pentecostal proclamation, resulting in three thousand new believers, Luke wrote, "Fear came upon every soul, and many wonders and signs were done through the apostles" (Acts 2:43). In Romans, Paul lamented a people who have "no fear of God before their eyes" (3:18). And in Revelation, John revealed who is worshipping around the throne—"Praise our God, all you His servants and those who fear Him" (19:5).

Heeding Malachi's call to fear the Lord does not mean I must walk around on eggshells living in constant fear that

God is going to put His hand of retribution on me. Rather, fearing God means to live with a conscious awareness of His presence, wanting to do nothing that might cause God to remove His hand of blessing and anointing from me. Malachi knew that living with this kind of awareness would make a difference in what we do, where we go, what we say, and how we live.

Malachi saw the coming day when Jesus, our Sun of Righteousness, would come and bring light from darkness, life from death, wholeness from sickness, freedom from bondage, and joy from sorrow. This Sun of Righteousness would come with "healing" in His outstretched wings. Jesus came and immersed the world in healing power. Early on in his gospel, Matthew recorded, "They brought to Him all sick people who were afflicted with various diseases and torments, and those who were demon-possessed, epileptics, and paralytics; and He healed them" (Matthew 4:24). As Jesus healed those who came to Him, He demonstrated that He has power not just to heal bodies but also to heal the sin-sick human heart.

Jesus came and immersed the world in healing power.

I am typing these words in the midst of a beautiful Texas Hill Country sunrise. As the sun rises, it brings light from the darkness of the night hours. As you look at it, it brings warmth to your face. And for those of us who fear the Lord, this Sun of Righteousness, our Lord Jesus, rises with healing in His wings, bringing light to our lives and warmth to our hearts. Jesus is here walking across the pages of Malachi. He is the Sun of Righteousness, and He still rises to meet us with healing in His wings.

34 FINDING JESUS IN MATTHEW

He Is the Christ, the Son of the Living God

[Jesus] said to them, "But who do you say that I am?"

Simon Peter answered and said, "You are the Christ, the Son of the living God."

—MATTHEW 16:15–16

*A*s we turn now to the Gospels in the New Testament, we find the written eyewitness accounts of Jesus, clothed in human flesh and walking the ways of our world. Matthew first met the Lord along the northern shore of the Sea of Galilee. He was a customs officer for the Roman government; not the most endearing of jobs for a Jewish citizen. He left his livelihood and followed after Jesus with abandonment. After the resurrection, he took pen in hand, and, inspired by the Holy Spirit, wrote the gospel that bears his name. He introduced Jesus as the "King of the Jews" (Matthew 2:2) and presented Him as the promised Messiah who had come to fulfill the prophecies of the Old Testament.

One of the unique approaches of our Lord was that He was always asking questions, not because He was needing answers, but because it was His way of getting us to see ourselves as we really are. In fact, the four Gospels record more than one hundred questions posed by Jesus. Matthew took note and recorded many of them for all posterity. Two of these questions came in rapid succession in a meeting with His disciples at Caesarea Philippi. The first, "Who do men say that I, the Son of Man, am?" (Matthew 16:13). In other words, "What is the polling data saying?" After all, many to this day make their decisions by waiting until they see which way the wind of public opinion is blowing before taking a decisive stand on a matter. It seems much of our world today is still more interested in what men say than in what God says.

Jesus quickly followed with one of the most pointed, penetrating, and personal questions He ever asked: "Who do *you* say that I am?" Public consensus must be laid aside. Christ's interest is in our personal conviction. The question is emphatic in the language of the New Testament. That is, it places the emphasis on the personal pronoun, *you*. Had we been sitting in the circle of disciples that evening we would have heard Jesus ask the question similar to this: "What about *you* . . . *you* and *you* only . . . *you* and no one else . . . *you* and *you* alone . . . Who do *you* say that I am?" God bless Simon Peter. He bore the brunt of more criticism than all the disciples put together. He was often so boastful. So it should be no surprise that it was Peter who proudly boasted that if all the followers of Christ forsook Him, he could still be counted on. His impulsiveness was on display when he cut off the ear of the servant of the high priest in Gethsemane's garden on the night of Christ's betrayal and arrest. But here, at Caesarea Philippi, Peter was inspired of the Holy Spirit, and immediately on the heels of Jesus' question, he blurted out the inspired truth, "You are the Christ, the Son of the Living God" (Matthew 16:16).

When Matthew recorded this pronouncement of Simon Peter, he used the strongest article in the Greek language to declare that Jesus was *the* Christ, *the* anointed One, *the* long-awaited Messiah of Israel. For the rest of his life, Peter insisted on this truth. He would meet his martyr's death by crucifixion. But declaring to his executioners that he was unworthy to be crucified in the same manner as his Lord, he requested to be crucified upside down. He gave his life insisting to the end that Jesus was "the Christ, the Son of the living God."

> Peter . . . blurted out the inspired truth, "You are the Christ, the Son of the Living God" (Matthew 16:16).

In Rome, the ancient Pantheon, the temple to all the gods, can be visited to this very day. It was there that the conquered people of the Roman Empire could go and worship at niches provided for the gods they served, whether they might be Jupiter or Juno or whomever. But the conquered followers of Christ refused to have a niche for Jesus beside the pagan gods of Jupiter, Juno, and the like. They said, "No, there is only one God and His name is Jesus." And they gave their lives by the hundreds of thousands for this truth.

Jesus is here in Matthew's gospel. On page after page, Matthew made it plain. This Jesus, who was crucified, buried, and risen from the dead is both Lord and Christ. And all those down through the centuries who have come to faith in Him have, in one way or another, echoed these words of Simon Peter: "You are the Christ, the Son of the living God."

35 FINDING JESUS IN MARK

He Is the God of the Second Touch

Then [Jesus] came to Bethsaida; and they brought a blind man to Him, and begged Him to touch him. So He took the blind man by the hand and led him out of the town. And when He had spit on his eyes and put His hands on him, He asked him if he saw anything. And he looked up and said, "I see men like trees, walking." Then He put His hands on his eyes again and made him look up. And he was restored and saw everyone clearly.

—MARK 8:22–25

*M*ost all of Jesus' recorded healing miracles in the Gospels were instantaneous. He simply spoke the word and healing happened. But here, in Mark's account of this blind man in Galilee, the healing is intentionally in two stages. Since physical sight is often a metaphor for understanding, Jesus' two-part healing was to reflect the gradual unveiling and understanding of the disciples. It was a miracle with an intended message for the disciples and for us.

When Jesus touched this blind man, he could see. But his vision was so blurry he could not tell if he was looking at a man or a tree. He said, "I can see! But I see men that look like trees walking." He couldn't see if the men were wearing glasses or not. He couldn't tell if they were wearing shirts or ties, or whether their shirttails were tucked in or untucked. He saw men, but his vision was so blurred, they looked like trees walking.

By the way, there were some other things he could not see. He couldn't see if eyes were tearful, if a face was dirty or a countenance distraught. He couldn't see if a brow was furrowed, if shoulders were stooped, feet were bare, or clothes were frayed. Therefore, if he could not see a man with a dirty face, he could not wash the face of the unclean man. If he couldn't see a tear in an eye, he couldn't bring comfort to a broken heart. If he couldn't see shoulders that were stooped, he couldn't lighten the load of the fellow traveler. If he couldn't see feet that were bare, he couldn't provide shoes for the needy individual. Through his blurry vision, he saw men who looked like trees walking.

A lot of us today are like this man—and, spiritually speaking, like the disciples—in need of a second touch so that we might see everyone clearly. There are men and women in our traffic patterns of life whose hair has turned gray in their declining years, who are wondering how they will pay their bills next month. We cross paths with those who have recently heard the doctor say, "You have cancer." We pass by those whose homes have been destroyed by betrayals and addictions. Our Lord Jesus came to earth not for a crowd but for each and every individual who is not only known to Him but also indescribably valuable to Him.

Every finger of every hand of every one of the billions alive on the planet right now has a different fingerprint. Every individual has a unique DNA. Every snowflake that falls in winter is different from every other one. Every star in the heavens, God calls by name. Every little field sparrow that falls to the ground is noted by our great God. Every single hair on your head is given a number by Him. Jesus doesn't look at the crowds; He looks at the individual. He looks at you. He looks at me. Preachers do not have congregations sitting in front of them, but rather collections of individuals with unique needs and heartaches and hurts. Teachers do not have a class sitting in front of them, but a set of individuals, each one valuable to God.

Mark recorded this story in the middle of his gospel to show us how much, like this blind man, we are in need of the second touch of our Lord. Until then we will continue through life seeing men, not as individuals who are individually loved by Jesus, but as "trees" walking around. This second healing touch is what enables us to see each other clearly through the eyes of Christ.

We find Jesus walking through every page of Mark's gospel. The good news for you and me is that He is still the God of the Second Touch.

36 FINDING JESUS IN LUKE

He Is the Third Person on the Emmaus Road

Two of them were traveling that same day to a village called Emmaus. . . . And they talked together of all these things which had happened. . . . While they conversed and reasoned, . . . Jesus Himself drew near and went with them. But their eyes were restrained, so that they did not know Him. . . . And beginning at Moses and all the Prophets, He expounded to them in all the Scriptures the things concerning Himself. . . . Then their eyes were opened and they knew Him; and He vanished from their sight.

—LUKE 24:13–16, 27, 31

*F*or three glorious years Christ's followers had lived with Him and learned from Him. But in such a short time, this came to an abrupt and crashing conclusion. He was viciously executed and His body placed in the cold, dark dampness of a tomb. All the disciples had forsaken Him and fled. Two of them, from the village of Emmaus, headed back home, lamenting, "We were hoping that it was He who was going to redeem Israel" (Luke 24:21). But that hope was buried in the tomb of Joseph of Arimathea outside the city walls of Jerusalem. Dejected and dismayed, they were walking proof that there is never any power in the present when there is no more hope in the future.

Then suddenly, the resurrected Christ appeared and began walking with them, though they "did not know Him" (v. 16). As they journeyed together, Jesus "expounded to them in all the Scriptures the things concerning Himself" (v. 27). The word *expounded* suggests something translated out of a foreign language. The Bible is like that. It is a foreign language to those who do not walk in the Spirit of Christ. After this incredible conversation with Jesus, the disciples' "eyes were opened" (v. 31), and they responded, "Did not our heart burn within us while He talked with us on the road, and while He opened the Scriptures to us?" (v. 32).

Jesus, "beginning at Moses and all the Prophets," revealed to them how He was in every book of the Bible. From the Pentateuch to the Prophets, Jesus preached Jesus on the Emmaus Road. From Moses to Malachi, He revealed how the entire Jewish Bible spoke of Him. As He taught them, a shadow of the cross fell across the Old Testament, and their "eyes were opened." *He* was that ram at Abraham's altar. *He* was that spotless Passover Lamb whose blood was shed to bring freedom from slavery and deliverance from death. *He* was that scarlet thread

> Jesus, "beginning at Moses and all the Prophets," revealed to them how He was in every book of the Bible.

hung out Rahab's window. And the Shepherd King David spoke so much about in his psalms? *He*, too, was the Lord Jesus. As these two disciples continued to listen, they understood that Jesus was Isaiah's suffering servant as well as the fourth man in the burning fiery furnace with Shadrach, Meshach, and Abed-Nego. No wonder their hearts burned within them while He talked with them and revealed the Scriptures to them along the road. And then, as mysteriously as He arrived, "He vanished from their sight" (Luke 24:31).

With beating, burning hearts, the disciples hurried back to Jerusalem, around the corners and down the narrow alleys they raced, up Mount Zion, finally to find the other disciples and share the good news: "'The Lord is risen indeed.' . . . And they told about the things that had happened on the road" (vv. 34–35).

One of these two disciples was named "Cleopas" (v. 18). The other was left unnamed. Perhaps he was unnamed so that you and I can find ourselves in this picture as we walk our very own Emmaus Road. If we have eyes to see, Jesus is with us, *right now*. If we have ears to hear, He still speaks to us along the way, by His Spirit and through His Word. And when we awaken to His truth, it just might be that we will join them in saying, "Did not our heart burn within us while He talked with us on the road, and while He opened the Scriptures to us?"

The two dejected and cold hearts of the Emmaus disciples were set on fire when Jesus revealed the meaning of the Scriptures to them. Things have not changed these past two millennia. The Bible is a sealed book until Jesus opens it to us. Those who do not know Him can gain a head knowledge of Him from the Bible, but they can never gain spiritual knowledge and truth without Him. We all need our eyes opened to the fact that He is still walking along beside us and still opening the truth of Scripture to us. Jesus is here in Luke. He was . . . and still is . . . the third person on our Emmaus Road.

37 FINDING JESUS IN JOHN

He Is the Resurrection and the Life

"I am the resurrection and the life. He who believes in Me, though he may die, he shall live. And whoever lives and believes in Me shall never die. Do you believe this?"

—JOHN 11:25–26

It was a sad and somber day in the small village of Bethany on the eastern slope of the Mount of Olives as Jesus stood with a brokenhearted family and their close friends at the grave of Lazarus. From His lips came an astonishing claim: "I am the resurrection and the life. He who believes in Me, though he may die, he shall live. And whoever lives and believes in Me shall never die." This one statement is among the boldest and most definitive acknowledgments of our Lord's deity. The resurrection is what separates Him from the thousand other gurus and prophets who have come down the pike. After declaring Himself to be the resurrection and the life, the Victor over death, He looks squarely into their faces—and ours—and asks life's bottom-line question: "Do you believe this?"

One of my personal frustrations in Scripture reading is that it is, like all other writings, linear. If we had a recording of His actual words, it would reveal so much more about where He placed His inflection for emphasis. Did He ask, "Do *you* believe this?" Did He ask, "Do you *believe* this?" Or perhaps He emphasized the last word in the question, "Do you believe *this*?"

Christ's question is intensely personal. Perhaps in driving home the fact that our salvation is a personal and individual matter, Jesus asked, "Do *you* believe this?" After all, when it comes to saving faith in the finished work of Christ, what really matters is not what your mother or father, husband or wife, or anyone else believes. It is the most personal of all life's questions. What about you? Do you believe that Christ's death and resurrection should be relegated to some *ancient* shelf of obscurity along with other ancient myths and fables? The question is personal. Do *you* believe this?

It might well be that as Jesus asked this question in the Bethany cemetery, His emphasis was placed on the word *believe*. "Do you *believe* this?" He is not interested in whether or not we were giving intellectual assent to His claims. He wants to know if we believe what He has said. That is, do we put our total trust and faith in Him and His words? With Jesus, the real issue is always one of faith. Jesus' question is not just personal, it is pointed: "Do you *believe* this?"

But now to the heart of the issue of His claim to being "the resurrection and the life." True faith must always rest on objective truth and fact. Most likely Jesus asked the question in this way: "Do you believe *this*?" In other words, He wants to know if we believe *this*—His claim of deity. When Jesus said, "I am," He captured the attention of all around. "I am" was God's own name that He revealed to Moses when He inquired of His name at the burning bush. God instructed Moses to tell the Israelites that "I AM has sent me to you" (Exodus 3:14). When Jesus said, "I am," all those listening recognized it to be an affirmation of His deity. Paul would later affirm this when he wrote, "He is the image of the invisible God" (Colossians 1:15). In John's gospel alone, he took note of an "I AM" statement by Jesus on seven different occasions. The question is not only personal and pointed, it is precise. "Do you believe *this*?"

But there is more. Jesus asked if we believe *this*—His claim about destiny. "Though he may die, he shall live" (John 11:25). Jesus means the body may indeed die, but not the spirit. There is a part of you that will live as long as God lives, which is forever and forever. There is another life that is a million times a million longer than this one, an eternity . . . with Him. Do you believe *this*? Jesus wants to know if you believe His claim about His own deity and your own destiny.

> Jesus wants to know if you believe His claim about His own deity and your own destiny.

There are a lot of questions we must face in life. Where will I attend college? What profession will I choose to engage? With whom will I spend the rest of my life in marriage? But there is only one major question in death—"Do you believe this?" Jesus prefaced this question with a declaration: "I am the resurrection and the life. He who believes in Me, though he may die, he shall live. And whoever lives and believes in Me shall never die." And then there is life's bottom-line question: Do you believe this? Settle the issue once and for all by joining Martha, Lazarus's sister, in professing, "Yes, Lord, I believe that *You* are the Christ, the Son of God" (John 11:27, emphasis added).

We find Jesus, the great I AM, walking through the pages of Luke—He is the Resurrection and the Life.

38 FINDING JESUS IN ACTS

*He Is the Shining Light on
the Road to Damascus*

*As he journeyed he came near Damascus, and suddenly a light shone
around him from heaven. Then he fell to the ground, and heard a
voice saying to him, "Saul, Saul, why are you persecuting Me?" And
he said, "Who are You, Lord?" Then the Lord said, "I am Jesus." . . .
So he, trembling and astonished, said, "Lord, what do You want me
to do?"*

—ACTS 9:3–6

*A*ll of us have experienced defining moments in our
lives, those snapshots in time when the course of
our lives took on a new direction or an added dimension. All
Scripture is equally inspired (2 Timothy 3:16), but there are
certain chapters that seem to stand as mountaintops above
the rest. One such chapter is the ninth chapter of Acts with
its startling account of the conversion of the apostle Paul on
the Damascus Road.

Terrorism in the Middle East is an all-too-common
event today. But it is nothing new. Saul of Tarsus was the
master terrorist of his day. And, like today, his terroristic
activity was all in the name of religion. He was on his way

to Damascus to put down an uprising of new believers in Christ who were gathering in that city. As he journeyed, he left behind a trail of blood and murder, all the while actually thinking he was doing it for God. We last encountered him in Scripture at the stoning of Stephen outside the Lions' Gate of the city of Jerusalem.

Saul of Tarsus was a Jew of Jews. He studied at the feet of Gamaliel, the leading rabbi of his time. His education was comparable to that which could be had from the most elite institutions of higher learning in the Western world today. He was a member of the Sanhedrin, the equivalent of the Supreme Court of the land. This new Christian movement, with claims that Jesus of Nazareth had risen from the grave, was sweeping through Israel with multiplied thousands of converts and presenting an alarming challenge to the Jewish faithful. It was a movement Saul felt compelled to stop. But after his conversion experience in Acts 9, Saul took on a new name, Paul, and from his pen poured out almost half of the New Testament.

Later when giving his conversion testimony, Paul said, "Suddenly a great light from heaven shone around me. And I fell to the ground" (Acts 22:6–7). Again and again, we are captured by this word, *suddenly*, in Scripture. On the day of Pentecost, "suddenly there came a sound from heaven" (2:2). What took place that day was not the result of process or development. It was not manifested by merit. It came *suddenly*. Remember the Bethlehem shepherds? "Suddenly" a great angelic choir announced the Savior's birth (Luke 2:13). Later, when Paul and Silas were in a Philippian jail, "suddenly" a violent earthquake opened the prison doors (Acts 16:26). And here on the road to Damascus, "suddenly" Jesus appeared to Paul in a great light from heaven (9:3). Oh, the possibilities if we would only live in the realm of expecting the unexpected—the *suddenly*—today. Often, when we least expect it, we, too, can be surprised by God Himself.

As Jesus appeared to Paul in a great shining light, Paul's immediate response was to ask two of life's most important questions. First, the question of *Who?*—"Who are You, Lord?" (v. 5). And second, the question of *What?*—

> Often, when we least expect it, we, too, can be surprised by God Himself.

"What do You want me to do?" (v. 6). Before we can ever find the answer to the second question, we must know for certain the answer to the first. Who is Jesus to you? Is He simply some great teacher, prophet, holy man? Or do you know Him to be who He said He was, the Messiah, the Christ who came "to seek and to save that which was lost" (Luke 19:10)? When Christ reigns and rules on the throne of your heart by faith, then and only then can you begin to find the purpose for which you were created and ask, "Lord, what do You want *me* to do?" Somewhere there is a job for you to do in His kingdom here on earth, something that no one else can do like you.

The Lord Jesus still has a way of showing up unexpectedly in our lives to bring us into the reality of His presence . . . and often, as with Saul of Tarsus, it's when we truly think we are doing something that is pleasing to Him. Perhaps He has not "suddenly" surprised you with some great shining light, but you've no doubt been surprised by God just the same. Perhaps it is time to ask, "Lord, who are You?" And when convinced He is who He said He was, to ask the second question, "Lord, what do You want me to do?" True success in life is finding the answer to this question, knowing His will for your life, and doing it!

Yes, Jesus is here in the words of Acts. He is the shining light on the road to Damascus—and in each of our lives today.

39 FINDING JESUS IN ROMANS

He Is Our Justifier

For whom He foreknew, He also predestined to be conformed to the image of His Son, that He might be the firstborn among many brethren. Moreover whom He predestined, these He also called; whom He called, these He also justified; and whom He justified, these He also glorified.

—ROMANS 8:29–30

It is one thing to be forgiven, but quite something else to be "justified." The word means to be declared to be right, to be made pure, as if we had never sinned. Christ is not our Justifier because we are worthy of being justified. We are worthy because we have been justified by Him through faith. It is not *our* works that justify us. It is *His* work—His finished work—on the cross that enables us to stand in His righteousness alone and one day to be presented faultless before His Father's throne. A human court of law may acquit someone of a crime. It can pardon someone from their trespasses. But a human court can never *justify* anyone's crime. But Jesus can and does because faith in Him is "accounted for righteousness" (Romans 4:5) to those who believe.

Justification is an important link in the chain of Christ's

redemptive process. There are five lengths in this chain presented in Romans 8:29–30, each of which is essential, and any one of which, if broken, destroys the entire chain of events. The first of these links expresses the *wisdom of God*: "For whom He foreknew." We get our English word *prognosis* from this compound Greek word meaning "to know before." God knows everything before it happens. Never once in the Gospels do we see Jesus coming upon a situation and exclaiming, "Wow, that was a surprise . . . I didn't see that one coming!" Christ has foreknowledge of all events yet to take place in our lives. He has seen it all before it happens. Nothing takes Him by surprise.

This truth leads us to the second length in the chain where we discover the *will of God*: Those He foreknew, "He also predestined to be conformed to the image of His Son." This word, *predestined*, comes from a preposition meaning "before" and a word meaning "horizon." That is to say, God marks out our boundaries beforehand. *Predestination* is one of the most misunderstood words in the Bible. While the word *election* deals with people, *predestination* deals with purposes. Here in our text, we are predestined to what? "To be conformed to the image of His Son."

Next comes a word about the *way of God*—"These He also called." God is the initiator. He foreknows, He predestines, then He calls us to Himself. There are two calls, the outward call and the inward call. The last invitation in the Bible says, "The Spirit and the bride say, 'Come!'" (Revelation 22:17). Who is the bride? The church, the bride of Christ. The church gives the outward call in a myriad of ways. But only the Spirit can issue the inward call to our hearts. How can two people sit on the same pew, in the same worship service, listen to the same sermon, in the same anointing, and one get up as if nothing mattered and the other fall under deep conviction of sin? The inner call of God to our hearts is what opens them to the truth of the gospel.

And now to the heart of the matter—"Whom He called, these He also justified." Here is the *work of God* on our behalf. He is our Justifier. He is the One who doesn't just forgive and cleanse us of our sin but who justifies it for us before the throne as if it never happened. What does this mean for me? Jesus is my Justifier. God put on my account the righteousness of His own pure Son. If I were to give you my Visa card and tell you to go out and buy whatever you wanted and put it on my account, that is exactly the same connotation of what we find in the word *justification*. God says, "Put it all on My account." He imputes Christ's own righteousness to me

> The church gives the outward call in a myriad of ways. But only the Spirit can issue the inward call to our hearts.

and in me, unworthy as I am. When God looks at you, He sees Jesus and His righteousness.

It's no wonder, then, that in the last link of this chain we see the *worship of God*—"Whom He justified, these He also glorified." Even as you and I wait for our final glorified state, the verb tense tells us that God already sees us as glorified. If there were no other word in the entire Bible about the eternal security of the believer, this one would be enough. Justification means we have been saved from the *penalty* of sin. Sanctification means we are being saved from the *power* of sin. And glorification means that one day we will be saved from the very *presence* of sin.

Paul's letter to the Romans is the greatest theological treatise in the Bible—and outside it as well. Every word of every verse of every chapter is filled with truth and meaning. We find Jesus here in Romans. He is our Justifier. He is the One who laid down His life and shed His blood for our justification. Paul framed it best when he said we were "*justified freely* by His grace through the redemption that is in Christ Jesus" (Romans 3:24, emphasis added).

40

FINDING JESUS IN FIRST CORINTHIANS

He Is the Bread and the Wine

For I received from the Lord that which I also delivered to you: that the Lord Jesus on the same night in which He was betrayed took bread; and when He had given thanks, He broke it and said, "Take, eat; this is My body which is broken for you; do this in remembrance of Me." In the same manner He also took the cup after supper, saying, "This cup is the new covenant in My blood. This do, as often as you drink it, in remembrance of Me."

—1 CORINTHIANS 11:23–25

*I*n our home we have an old family photo album that has been passed down through the decades. If you were to browse through it, most likely it would not have much meaning for you. There is a picture of my old home place on Crenshaw Street in Fort Worth with the white picket fence. To this day I carry on my leg a scar from the time I disobeyed my father and tried to scale over it. There is also the little house we moved into after our wedding. It was a small three-room house, behind a house, with no heat except an electric heater we moved from room to room. Many a morning we would wake to see ice formed on the inside of some of those windows. And then, of course, there are pictures of grandparents, relatives, and friends from across the years. That old album would mean little to you. But when I open its pages and wander through them, it stirs memories of the joy and happiness of our life journey.

Just as my family photo album arouses memories of the past, so do the elements of the communion table—the bread and the wine—evoke memories for those of us who have been born again into God's family. Jesus instructed us to remember Him when we share communion together. We refer to it as the "Lord's Supper" for a reason. It is His. Not mine, not ours. Thus He does the inviting, and we are His invited guests to His table, just as the disciples in the Upper Room were the evening of that last supper.

> We refer to it as the "Lord's Supper" for a reason. It is His. Not mine, not ours.

Across the centuries from prison cells to palace halls, from the catacombs in Rome, to believers hidden in house churches, to those gathered in high-steeple, stained-glass sanctuaries in the Western world, anyone, anywhere who comes to the Lord's Table is welcome upon their professed faith in Christ. And whenever and wherever believers gather for communion, this passage from Paul to the Corinthians is read and expounded upon. He had "received from the Lord" (1 Corinthians 11:23) that which he delivered to them and to us. Accompanying these apostolic words are four important reminders.

First, at the Lord's Table there is a *word of explanation*. Paul insisted that he was simply passing on what he had "received from the Lord." The Lord's Supper and baptism are the two ordinances of the church in which the gospel is clearly presented. In the act of baptism by immersion, we see pictured plainly the death, burial, and resurrection of the Lord. In communion, we see His body—broken for us—in the breaking of the unleavened bread. And in the cup— the rich, red fruit of the vine—we see a vivid picture of His blood shed for the remission of sins. Jesus said, "This is My body. . . . This cup is the new covenant in My blood" (vv. 24–25).

Approaching the Lord's Table, we also note a *word of exaltation*. The Bible says, "When He had given thanks" (v. 24), He broke the bread and passed it to His followers. Times of communion call for thankful hearts. We do not partake of the Lord's Supper to remind Him of anything, but to remember Him. We are a thankful people.

When we receive the bread and the cup, we are also expressing a *word of expectation*. Paul said, "For as often as you eat this bread and drink this cup, you proclaim the Lord's death till He comes" (v. 26). The Lord's Supper is not just a look backward, but a look forward. He is coming again.

When I travel, I take a picture of my wife, Susie, and I usually place it on the nightstand in my hotel room. But I don't do that at home. Why? Because I have her physical presence there. In our dispensation, while He is absent physically, we remember Him with the bread and the cup. But, one day, He is coming again, and we will put away this picture of Him when we "see Him as He is" (1 John 3:2).

Finally, there is a *word of examination*. Paul continued, "But let a man examine himself, and so let him eat of the bread and drink of the cup" (1 Corinthians 11:28). Times of communion can be seasons of refreshing in the presence of the Lord when we use them to examine ourselves and to find cleansing and a new beginning through confession and repentance.

How long has it been since you opened your own spiritual photo album? The bread and the cup stir up warm and wonderful memories for every believer of the time they came to know Him. For to know Him is to know life, abundant and eternal. We find Jesus here in Paul's first letter to those at Corinth . . . He is the Bread and the Wine.

41 FINDING JESUS IN SECOND CORINTHIANS

He Is the Ultimate Authority

For we must all appear before the judgment seat of Christ, that each one may receive the things done in the body, according to what he has done, whether good or bad.

—2 CORINTHIANS 5:10

*P*erhaps there is no other subject that has been relegated to the back recesses and corners of our minds more than the fact that each of us will one day stand before the supreme Judge of all the earth. In His court there are no mistrials, no appeals, no probations, no adjudicated sentences, and no hung juries. His is the one court where ultimate and perfect justice will prevail.

The subject of a final judgment for each person who has ever lived is one of much confusion for many believers. However, when we understand that there are different judgments delineated in the Bible, it brings focus and greater understanding to what lies ahead for us. So, here comes the Judge.

The first judgment related to us has already taken place. It is the *judgment of sin*, the believer's sin. Jesus said, "He who hears My word and believes in Him who sent Me has everlasting life, and shall not come into judgment, but has passed from death into life" (John 5:24). Talk about some good news—here it is! God judged the believer's sin one dark day outside the city walls of Jerusalem when "[God] made Him [Christ] who knew no sin to be sin for us" (2 Corinthians 5:21). And this is why Paul could confidently say, "There is therefore now *no* condemnation [judgment] to those who are in Christ Jesus" (Romans 8:1, emphasis added).

There is the *judgment of sinners*, known as the "Great White Throne Judgment" (Revelation 20:11), awaiting all those who lived and died without trusting Christ as their personal Savior. John was the only apostle who did not meet a martyr's death. At over ninety years of age, he was exiled to the lonely island of Patmos by the Romans. There, God opened up heaven to him and showed him what was to come. Inspired by the Spirit of God, John carefully wrote what he saw: "I saw a great white throne and Him who sat on it, from whose face the earth and the heaven fled away. And there was found no place for them. And I saw the dead, small and great, standing before God, and books were opened. . . . And anyone not found written in the Book of Life was cast into the lake of fire" (vv. 11–12, 15).

Every lost person who has ever lived will stand before Christ to give account of their lives. These lost souls will be pronounced guilty at the Great White Throne and cast into a godless eternity of darkness. Lost beyond hope, lost beyond help, lost beyond time. Lost, forever lost.

But for those of us who have placed our trust in Christ alone, there is great news. We will stand before the "judgment seat of Christ" at the *judgment of the saints.* At this judgment, taking place immediately after the return of Christ, our works will be judged, not our sins. Our sins were judged on the cross when Christ took the judgment we deserved for us. Here, at the judgment seat the degree of our rewards will be determined by the One who judges all things well.

At this judgment of the saints, an amazing thing happens. When we stand before Christ, our judge, He steps down from the judge's bench, comes to stand by our side, and begins to plead our case for us. As the apostle John said, "We have an Advocate [lawyer] with the Father, Jesus Christ the righteous" (1 John 2:1). Christ—our Advocate, our own personal defense attorney—will plead our case before the judgment bar. And the good news is that God cannot and will not see our sins because of the blood of Jesus, which has been applied to our lives by His grace and through our faith.

> At the judgment seat the degree of our rewards will be determined by the One who judges all things well.

We find Jesus here in 2 Corinthians;

He is our faithful judge. Christ is coming to judge the world. The Lord Jesus is the only true and righteous Judge. Not a single one of us can really stand in judgment of someone else's heart. Ultimately, we can rest in the truth of Genesis 18:25: "Shall not the Judge of all the earth do right?"

Take a moment to be still and meditate on the wonderful privilege we believers in Christ have coming our way. We have an "Advocate with the Father," and His sweet name is Jesus. When all is said and done, the only question that really matters in this world—or the next—is this one: Is my name in the book? Because here comes the Judge! *He* is the ultimate authority.

42 FINDING JESUS IN GALATIANS

He Is the One Who Lives in Me

I have been crucified with Christ; it is no longer I who live, but Christ lives in me; and the life which I now live in the flesh I live by faith in the Son of God, who loved me and gave Himself for me.

—GALATIANS 2:20

As a seventeen-year-old teenager who could count on one hand the times I had ever been inside a church, I came to know Christ as my personal Savior. For me, it was like going from darkness into light. I knew something grand and glorious had taken place in me. Instantly, I began to love what I used to hate and hate what I used to love. I remember asking one of my new Christian friends, "What happened to me?" He pointed me to Galatians 2:20. I memorized it that day, and across the decades I have held it close to my heart as one of my life verses.

Like bees on a honeycomb, this verse swarms with seven personal pronouns. This single verse is perhaps the most complete and intensely personal description of the Christian life to be found in the New Testament. "Christ lives in me!" Think of that four-monosyllable statement. What an awesome thought. This great Creator God has come to take up residence in me. This is the very essence of the Christian life. The Lord Jesus is alive—right this very moment—in me!

> This is the very essence of the Christian life. The Lord Jesus is alive—right this very moment—in me!

Galatians 2:20 reveals three important things Christ has done for us. First, He took something from us—our old life. Paul said, "I have been crucified with Christ." We hear a lot about how Christ was crucified *for* us. But the apostle went beyond this to reveal that we were crucified *with* Christ. As the Lord Jesus hung on Calvary's cross, those in the crowd saw only one man on that center cross. But God the Father saw not just Christ but you and me and all others who would place their trust in Him hanging with Him on that center cross. When we come to Christ, God takes our old life from us. We are "crucified with Christ." In the first-century world, a person carrying a cross meant only one thing: he was on his way to die. The call of the faith is to take up our own cross and live like dead men and women today, dead to our old lives and alive to a new life in Christ.

The Lord Jesus also put something in us: our new life in Him. "It is no longer I who live, but Christ lives in me" (Galatians 2:20). Our new life in Christ is not a reformed life. It is not an improved life. It is not even a changed life. It is an *exchanged* life. We give God our old life, and He gives us one that is brand-new. Stop and meditate again for a moment on this incredible thought: "Christ lives in me." There is no way to defeat those who believe that Christ is truly alive today and has come to take up permanent residency in our lives.

But there is more. Paul continued by saying that He gave something for us: His own life. "[He] loved me and gave Himself for me" (v. 20). There are two realities I wish the entire world could know: God loves us, and Christ gave Himself for us. In the language of the New Testament, these two verbs are punctiliar in nature, simply meaning that at a single point in time God's great love took Him to the cross, and there He willingly "gave Himself for us."

Think of it . . . "[He] loved me." If we could ask Paul how we could know Jesus loves us, he would fire back without batting an eye, "He gave Himself for me." Jesus didn't just speak platitudes about His love. He proved His love. He died in my place. He took my sin so that I could take His right-eousness. His love led Him to die my death so I could live His life. He "gave Himself for me!" What a Savior!

This letter to the people who lived in the region of Galatia was one of the great apostle's first letters written soon after his first missionary journey. We find Jesus here in Galatians. He is the One who promises never to leave or forsake us. He is the One who lives in me . . . and you, if you have placed your trust in Him alone.

43 FINDING JESUS IN EPHESIANS

He Is Our Unsearchable Riches

To me, who am less than the least of all the saints, this grace was given, that I should preach among the Gentiles the unsearchable riches of Christ.

—EPHESIANS 3:8

*L*aced throughout Paul's letter to the Ephesians is the concept of the "riches" of Christ. He said, "In Him we have redemption through His blood, the forgiveness of sins, according to the riches of His grace" (Ephesians 1:7). Next, Paul stated his desire that your understanding would be enlightened "that you may know what is the hope of His calling, what are the riches of the glory of His inheritance in the saints" (v. 18). He continued, "But God, who is rich in mercy, . . . raised us up together . . . in the heavenly places in Christ Jesus, that in the ages to come He might show the exceeding riches of His grace in His kindness toward us in Christ Jesus" (2:4, 6–7). Paul then prayed "that He would grant you, according to the riches of His glory, to be strengthened with might through His Spirit in the inner man" (3:16).

The subject of Paul's preaching to the Gentiles was what He called "the unsearchable riches of Christ" (v. 8). He lists these "unsearchable riches" in Ephesians 1:7: "In Him we have redemption through His blood, the forgiveness of sins, according to the riches of His grace." In this one verse, we have the essence of apostolic preaching in the New Testament. It begins with the phrase "in Him." What Christ has to offer is not about religion or ritual; it is about a relationship, a vibrant, personal relationship with Him. What He offers us is "in Him."

Life is about relationships. The bottom line is we will never be in a proper relationship with others until we are in a proper relationship with ourselves. And this will never happen until we discover how valuable we are to Christ by entering into a personal relationship with and "in Him."

These riches of which Paul preached reveal to us that "we have redemption" (Ephesians 1:7). *Right now.* The verb Paul used here is in the present, active, indicative form, meaning that the redemption is occurring in actual time right now. We don't need to wait for redemption. We have it "in Him." Much of our world is looking for immediate gratification, but true gratification comes in discovering the unsearchable riches of Christ. And we can know that in the here and now.

The message of Paul that we are "in Him" and that "we have redemption" came at an expensive cost. The next phrase in his message of the riches of Christ reveals this truth: "through His blood." Christ's riches come to us at a great

> Christ's riches come to us at a great price, but they can be ours without cost or condition on our part.

price, but they can be ours without cost or condition on our part. It is not by His power or His love or His teaching but by His blood that He has purchased a way for us to be in relationship with the Father. This privilege is neither earned nor deserved and cannot be bought. It is a gift given freely to us through the sacrifice of Jesus' blood. We need only believe and follow.

And the result? "The forgiveness of sins." It is only through Christ that we can find forgiveness for our sin. Then, as the psalmist promised, "As far as the east is from the west, so far has He removed our transgressions from us" (Psalm 103:12). We should be eternally grateful that God's promise is from the east to the west and not from the north to the south. North and south both have an end. There is a North Pole and a South Pole. However, east and west know no end; they simply continue on. God removes our sins from us forever.

Paul said all of this good news is "according to the riches of His grace" (Ephesians 1:7). Note Paul's words carefully. It is "according to" and not "out of" the riches of His grace. If I were to give you a dollar bill, I would be giving you "out of" my riches. But if I were to hand you a blank check with my signature affixed to it, for you to use as you will, I would be giving to you "according to" my riches. God is rich in His grace and mercy toward us. He freely gives to us "according to the riches of His grace." These riches come to us through the sacrifice of Jesus: "For you know the grace of our Lord Jesus Christ, that though He was rich, yet for your sakes He became poor, that you through His poverty might become rich" (2 Corinthians 8:9).

The *something* many of us think we need is really *Someone*. And His sweet name is Jesus. We find Him here in Paul's letter to those in the region of Ephesus. Jesus was, He is, and He forever will be our "unsearchable riches."

44 FINDING JESUS IN PHILIPPIANS

He Is Our Prize

Brethren, I do not count myself to have apprehended; but one thing I do, forgetting those things which are behind and reaching forward to those things which are ahead, I press toward the goal for the prize of the upward call of God in Christ Jesus.

—PHILIPPIANS 3:13–14

Paul's letter to the believers in Philippi is packed with one spiritual nugget after another. We catch a glimpse of the apostle's heart when we hear him say the following:

- "For to me, to live is Christ, and to die is gain" (Philippians 1:21).
- "At the name of Jesus every knee should bow . . . and . . . every tongue should confess that Jesus Christ is Lord, to the glory of God the Father" (2:10–11).
- "That I may know Him and the power of His resurrection, and the fellowship of His sufferings, being conformed to His death" (3:10).
- "I can do all things through Christ who strengthens me" (4:13).

No other New Testament letter contains the razor-sharp focus on what Paul called "the prize," which he identifies as "the upward call of God," which is found in Christ Jesus our Lord. In Philippians, Jesus is our Prize.

Focus. That one single word holds the key to success in so many endeavors of life. We find this at the center of Paul's own interests through his letters. In Colossians, he challenges us to "set your mind on things above" (Colossians 3:2). It is also at the very heart of his message to the Philippians, when he said, "This one thing I do" (Philippians 3:13 KJV). The ability to obtain and then maintain focus is one of the key elements necessary for spiritual growth in the Christian life. Keeping Christ, our Prize, in the center of our lives will lead us to do four very important things:

1. *Focusing on our Prize will keep our priorities in order.* Paul said, "This one thing I do." Not ten things. Not five things. Not even two things. But this *one* thing I do. Focus will keep our priorities in order. Once we have defined our goal, our goal will then begin to define us.

2. *Focusing on Jesus, our Prize, will give us a forward-looking mind-set that is vitally important to spiritual growth.* Too many of us are prone to spending too much time looking around us, or worse, looking

behind us at past mistakes or past victories. Paul challenged us to reach "forward to those things which are ahead." Focusing on Jesus will lead us to a wise forgetfulness about our past and will enable us to continue to make sure our reach exceeds our grasp.

3. *Keeping Jesus as our focus will bring a fresh passion to our lives, instilling within us a desire to do what is required of us . . . and then some.* Paul expressed it like this: "I press." This word *press* carries with it an intensity, much like an avid hunter who never gives up when pursuing his prey. Paul was able to "press toward the goal" because he had focus; he had "one thing" as the main priority of his life.

4. *Finally, focus brings us the ability to know where we are headed.* Paul said he was pressing toward what? "The goal." This Greek word is the foundation of our English word *scope*. Like the scope on a rifle, focus enables us to set our goals and priorities in the crosshairs. It allows us to know where we are going and how we are going to get there.

Focus—seeing Jesus as our Prize—is the source of successful living. It helps us begin our tasks with the end in mind. What is the goal toward which you are striving? What is in the crosshairs of your scope? When we begin to focus on Christ alone, we find that He will put our priorities in order, He will give us a forward look, He will bring a new passion to our lives, and He will let us clearly see the end from the beginning.

We find Jesus here in Philippians. He is our Prize. He alone should be in the crosshairs of our scope. Keep your life in focus by seeing Jesus as your Prize. And when you do, you will be able to say with Paul, "I can do all things through Christ who strengthens me" (Philippians 4:13). And then the reality of his truth will become personal to you as you join him in saying, "For to me, to live is Christ, and to die is gain" (Philippians 1:21).

FINDING JESUS IN COLOSSIANS

He Is the Creator God

He is the image of the invisible God, the firstborn over all creation. For by Him all things were created that are in heaven and that are on earth, visible and invisible, whether thrones or dominions or principalities or powers. All things were created through Him and for Him. And He is before all things, and in Him all things consist.

—COLOSSIANS 1:15–17

Most believers begin the story of Jesus far too late. When speaking of His beginning, many of us talk of Bethlehem and that star-filled night when Christ was born of the Virgin Mary in a smelly, Middle Eastern stable because there was no room for them in the inn. Then we proceed to tell of His life, His death and resurrection, and the promise of His return to take us home to heaven with Him. But in these words of Paul to the Colossians, we find one of the most incredible statements in all the Bible. They take us back before Bethlehem, back even before creation, back into the eternal counsels of God before time began. Paul spoke about Jesus not only as the "image of the invisible God," but he said, "By Him all things were created. . . . He is before all things." We find Jesus here in Colossians, and we find Him as the great Creator God Himself.

Paul referred to our Lord as the "image of the invisible God." The Greek word we translate into *image* is the same word from which we derive our English word *icon*. Jesus is the very portrait of God. If you want to know what God is like and looks like, just open your New Testament and look at Jesus. He is the *icon*, the picture, the express image of God. John echoed this truth in his own gospel when he said, "In the beginning was the Word, and the Word was with God, and the Word was God" (John 1:1). And so there would be zero chance of misunderstanding the identity of the One of whom he spoke, John continued, "And the Word became flesh and dwelt among us, and we beheld His glory" (v. 14). The writer of Hebrews also added that in these last days God has spoken to us by His Son who is "the express image of His person" (v. 3).

Jesus did not just appear on the scene in Bethlehem. He has been here all along. When we read in the initial verse of the Bible, "In the beginning God created the heavens and the earth" (Genesis 1:1), we find Jesus there. We should not think in terms of Genesis 1:1 as being the beginning of everything. It wasn't. "In the beginning was the Word," and the Word is Jesus. When we read Genesis 1:1 in the original Hebrew, we find the word *Elohim*, which we translate as "God." The significance of this word is that it is in the plural form, thus hinting in these first words of the Bible that God is really three persons in one: Father, Son, and Holy Spirit. Interestingly, the verb *created*, which follows this noun, is singular, seemingly making a mockery of grammar. Yet it should be in the singular form since *Elohim* is one God, the great Three in One. We see this truth revealed later in Genesis 1:26 when we read, "Let *Us* make man in *Our* image" (emphasis added). Thus, we can see the truth of Paul's words when he wrote, "By [Jesus] all things were created" (Colossians 1:16).

Jesus was there in creation. In fact, He is the Creator God Himself. There is a huge difference between creating something and making something. Many of us have *made* things, but not a single one of us has ever *created* something out of nothing. A cabinet maker may make a beautiful piece of furniture out of wood. However, he is totally inept at creating the wood itself.

> Jesus was there in creation. In fact, He is the Creator God Himself.

This physical universe was spoken into existence by Jesus. And when He created mankind, He gave every individual— out of the billions who have ever lived, do live, and will live—a thumbprint and a DNA that is completely unique. That kind of creativity is not possible without a Creator who sees you as indescribably valuable. And you were not just created *by* Him but "*for*

Him" (Colossians 1:16, emphasis added). You are someone very special to Jesus.

In his letter to the Colossians, Paul reached the apex of his argument when he declared, "In Him all things consist" (1:17). Jesus is not only our Creator, He is our sustainer. He holds it all together. The perfect tense of the verb here indicates that He continues to hold all things together, and apart from His doing so, everything would virtually disintegrate. Jesus is holding the very breath you are breathing as you read these pages right now. When we truly grasp what Paul has said here in Colossians, we will cease searching anywhere else for true purpose and meaning in life. It is only found in Jesus.

We find Jesus here in the Colossian letter. He is our great Creator God.

46 FINDING JESUS IN FIRST AND SECOND THESSALONIANS

He Is Our Soon-Coming King

But I do not want you to be ignorant, brethren, concerning those who have fallen asleep, lest you sorrow as others who have no hope. For if we believe that Jesus died and rose again, even so God will bring with Him those who sleep in Jesus. For this we say to you by the word of the Lord, that we who are alive and remain until the coming of the Lord will by no means precede those who are asleep. For the Lord Himself will descend from heaven with a shout, with the voice of an archangel, and with the trumpet of God. And the dead in Christ will rise first. Then we who are alive and remain shall be caught up together with them in the clouds to meet the Lord in the air. And thus we shall always be with the Lord.

—1 THESSALONIANS 4:13–17

There is no greater chasm between the early church in Acts and the modern twenty-first-century church than in how we each view the second coming of the Lord Jesus Christ. When was the last time you heard a message on this great and climactic event in human history? The subject of Christ's return has been virtually forgotten in modern church preaching and teaching. And yet, it was constantly on the minds and lips of the early believers. In the New Testament, the Second Coming is referred to more than any other subject and is prominently mentioned with over three hundred references. *Maranatha* (the Lord is coming) was the word constantly upon their lips. The early church greeted each other with this word. They comforted one another in their distress with this word. They shouted this word to their friends hanging from their crosses of execution and burning from the stakes of martyrdom. They arose every single morning and pillowed their heads each night looking for their soon-coming King.

For many in today's modern church, talk of future prophecies on God's timetable of the last days draws raised eyebrows, glassy eyes, and wide, even verbal yawns. When believers lose their hope of the future, they resort to having no power in the present. One of the primary reasons for today's lack of evangelistic fervor is the lack of anticipation, of being ready for Christ's return. It also results in an alarming lack of holiness and personal purity as, increasingly, life is lived with little to no urgency of being ready to meet the Lord in that unexpected moment when He comes again.

This is at the essence of Paul's letter to those in Thessalonica. In these letters, he built for them—and for us—a solid theological foundation for life now and the one to come. He wanted none of his readers to be "ignorant" concerning these things. Paul emphasized that the basis of the believer's hope is found in the fact and in their belief that "Jesus died and rose again." And then he described with vivid imagery how we will be "caught up" to meet the Lord in the air when He returns to rapture His church. The Greek word translated as "caught up" means to steal or to seize, to snatch away by violent force. And then Paul followed with one of the most assuring promises in all the Bible: "And thus we shall always be with the Lord."

> Paul . . . described with vivid imagery how we will be "caught up" to meet the Lord in the air when He returns.

Here in Thessalonians we are reminded that we have a soon-coming King. Paul drove four strong stakes into the ground of revelation regarding His coming. First, it is Christ Himself who will descend from heaven, just as He promised in the Upper Room when He declared, "If I go and prepare a place for you, I will come again and receive you to Myself; that where I am, there you may be also" (John 14:3). Yes, Jesus will descend from heaven just as the angel promised at His ascension, saying, "Men of Galilee, why do you stand gazing up into heaven? This same Jesus, who was taken up from you into heaven, will so come in like manner as you saw Him go into heaven" (Acts 1:11). Second, Jesus will return with a loud shout and with the voice of an archangel and with the trumpet of God blasting forth. Next, all those who have died in Christ will rise first from their graves to meet Him in the air. Finally, those of us who are alive at this great event will be miraculously changed and caught up with them in the air to meet the Lord and be ushered away into the endless ages of eternity. No wonder Paul concluded this paragraph by saying, "Therefore comfort one another with these words" (1 Thessalonians 4:18).

So what are we to do in anticipation of the return of the Lord Jesus Christ? We are to wait, watch, and work. James said to wait, to "be patient, brethren, until the coming of the Lord" (James 5:7). Paul said to watch by constantly "looking for the blessed hope and glorious appearing of our great God and Savior Jesus Christ" (Titus 2:13). And, at the end of his discourse on the resurrection and the Second Coming to those in Corinth, Paul admonished us all to work as we wait and watch when he wrote, "Therefore, my beloved brethren, be steadfast, immovable, always abounding in the work of the Lord, knowing that your labor is not in vain in the Lord" (1 Corinthians 15:58).

We find Jesus here in Paul's letters to the Thessalonians. He is our soon-coming King. *Maranatha* . . . the Lord is coming!

47 FINDING JESUS IN FIRST AND SECOND TIMOTHY

He Is the Mediator Between God and Man

For there is one God and one Mediator between God and men, the Man Christ Jesus.

—1 TIMOTHY 2:5

*M*ediation is a hot topic in our world today. A *mediator* is one who brings disputing parties together and works toward a reasonable solution to the conflict. Mediators are used in government, business, marriages, and many other venues where conflicts need to be resolved.

Conflict will tear your team apart. Whether it is at home, in the office, on the court, or even in the church, unresolved conflicts can do irreparable damage. The truth is, wherever you find two individuals, you will often find the need for effective conflict resolution. People have lost their jobs, marriages have been broken, and churches have split right down the middle simply because those involved have never learned the secrets of conflict resolution. And while disagreements are inevitable in life, they don't have to be destructive.

Those who solve their differences and resolve their

conflicts employ four valuable principles that, when put into practice, can have positive and productive results. First, effective mediators know there is a time to back off. They are wise enough to know that when tensions arise, the best approach is to step back and listen. They have learned that you never have to take back what you don't say. Second, those skilled in mediating conflicts also know there is a time to take a stand for what they know to be right. Third, skilled mediators realize there is a time to give in—to lose a few little skirmishes that don't really matter in the larger scheme of things—in order to win a bigger war. And lastly, they know there is a time to reach out, to take the initiative in extending a hand of reconciliation.

Of all the many names for Jesus in the Bible, one we should hold close to our hearts is this one used in Paul's letter to Timothy: the "one Mediator between God and men" (1 Timothy 2:5). There is no other. On almost every page of the Gospels, we find Jesus mediating conflicts. In Mark's gospel alone, we find others in conflict with Him on twenty-six different occasions. There was conflict in His own hometown of Nazareth. There was conflict with His own family, some of whom even sought to distance themselves from Him. There was constant conflict with the religious Pharisees. There was conflict with His best friends. Everywhere Jesus' sandaled feet took Him along the dusty roads of Judea and

Galilee, conflict seemed to swirl around Him. And in every instance, we find Him attempting to mediate those conflicts and reconcile others to God.

Consider humanity's relationship with God. We were in conflict with Him, with His purpose and plan for our lives. We had a good start in a perfect paradise. But we chose to go our own way and do our own thing. All of us—"for all have sinned and fall short of the glory of God" (Romans 3:23). Then Jesus came, our personal Mediator, to resolve our conflict and bring us into a restored relationship with the Father.

As the greatest Mediator, Jesus perfectly employed the elements of conflict resolution Himself. First, He backed off. See Him in Gethsemane's garden? In His darkest hour, we find Him backing off, kneeling down beneath those ancient and gnarled olive trees, listening to His heart, and surrendering to His Father's will.

Next, we find Him standing up. And, my, did He stand up! Before Caiaphas, the high priest. Before Herod, the puppet king. Before Pilate, the Roman procurator. When asked if He was indeed the Son of God, Jesus boldly proclaimed, "You rightly say that I am" (Luke 22:70).

> As the greatest Mediator, Jesus perfectly employed the elements of conflict resolution.

Then Jesus gave in. He had a goal

in mind: to restore the broken relationship between us and God. So He gave in. He was not pushed or shoved or kicked up the Via Dolorosa on the way to His place of execution. He went "as a lamb to the slaughter" (Isaiah 53:7). Willingly, Jesus laid down His life.

And finally, Jesus reached out. In your own mind's eye, can you see Him? He is suspended between earth and heaven on a Roman cross. His arms are outstretched in welcome, imploring you and me to be "reconciled to God" (Romans 5:10). With one hand, He reaches up to the Father and takes His hand. With the other, He reaches down to you and takes your hand into His own nailed-scarred one. And then? He takes your hand and places it in the hand of God. Talk about conflict resolution. Jesus is the epitome of it. In fact, He wrote the book on it—the Bible is the greatest continuous story of conflict resolution ever written.

No wonder Paul wrote to Timothy and declared there is one, and only one, "Mediator between God and men, the Man Christ Jesus" (1 Timothy 2:5). We find Jesus here in Timothy . . . He is the eternal Mediator between God and man.

48 FINDING JESUS IN TITUS

He Is Our Blessed Hope

For the grace of God that brings salvation has appeared to all men, teaching us that, denying ungodliness and worldly lusts, we should live soberly, righteously, and godly in the present age, looking for the blessed hope and glorious appearing of our great God and Savior Jesus Christ.

—TITUS 2:11–13

*A*s we read in Paul's letters to the Thessalonians, the early church lived in light of the return of Jesus Christ. They had been eyewitnesses to His resurrection and ascension. They had seen the miracle of His ascent from the Mount of Olives as He was lifted from the mountain and ascended up through the clouds and out of their sight on His journey back into heaven, leaving them with the parting promise that He "will so come in like manner" (Acts 1:11). They lived for that moment. In their hearts and minds it was imminent. He was coming back at any moment. They were not just ready for His return; they were consumed with wild anticipation as they earnestly and eagerly were "looking for and hastening the coming of the day of God" (2 Peter 3:12).

It is one thing to get ready for someone who is coming to

visit and quite another to eagerly anticipate their arrival. As a boy, I remember when my great-aunt would come to our home for a visit. We spent a day getting ready for her arrival. We made sure the house was clean and in proper order. We went grocery shopping to make sure we had the foods she enjoyed eating. But I never really eagerly anticipated her visits. I always had to be on my best behavior. She was quite boring, and as I type these words, I can still smell the mustiness of her dresses. We got ready for her arrival, all right, but without much eager anticipation on my part.

But things changed during my college years when Susie, now my wife, would come on those visits from Austin to Fort Worth to spend weekends in my parents' home. We spent considerable time getting ready for her. But words are useless for describing the anticipation, the eagerness that preceded those visits on my part. The hands on the clock never seemed to move slower than they did as I anxiously and eagerly awaited her arrival.

The hope held deep in the hearts of the New Testament believers was similar to this. It carried with it not just a sense of the importance of being ready for Christ's return but an eager anticipation of that moment. They lived with a constant longing, looking for the glorious appearing of their "blessed hope."

As days have turned into months, months into years,

years into decades, and decades into centuries, believers today have lost much of this anticipation. Little do those who see no signs of His return today realize that they have become signs themselves. I have witnessed several of these signs of Jesus' return with my own eyes. One Bible sign is to watch for a *providential people*, the Jews. Moses predicted that the Lord would "scatter [the Jews] among the peoples" and they would have no "resting place" (Deuteronomy 4:27; 28:65). But Ezekiel saw the day when God would "gather [His people] out of all countries, and bring [them] back into [their] own land" (Ezekiel 36:24). We are watching this miracle happen in our own lifetimes.

We are also called to keep our eyes on a *particular place*. Before Christ returns, the Bible says the little nation of Israel will once again become a major player on the world stage. After centuries of expulsion from their land, God has kept His promise to "bring back the captives of My people Israel" into their homeland once again (Amos 9:14). My own generation has witnessed the rebuilding of the state of Israel on the heels of the Holocaust when one out of every three Jews in the world were annihilated in Hitler's gas chambers. For the first time in 2,500 years, since the days of

> Before Christ returns, the Bible says the little nation of Israel will once again become a major player on the world stage.

Nebuchadnezzar and the Babylonian captivity, the children of Israel are ruling their own country from their own capital of Jerusalem.

We are also to watch for a *polluted pulpit.* One of the signs that our "blessed hope" is near is that "the time will come when they will not endure sound doctrine . . . and they will turn their ears away from the truth" (2 Timothy 4:3–4). We live in such a day. Denominations are dying. Many pulpits no longer preach that Jesus is "the way, the truth, and the life" (John 14:6).

These are but three of the many signs that Christ's coming may be imminent. These signs should cause us, like our Christian forefathers of old, to be eagerly and earnestly anticipating His coming again.

All people are in need of hope, and Jesus is the personification of that hope. We find Him here in Titus. He is our "blessed hope." And He is coming again to receive us unto Himself.

49 FINDING JESUS IN PHILEMON

He Is Our Friend Who Sticks Closer Than a Brother

For perhaps he departed for a while for this purpose, that you might receive him forever, no longer as a slave but more than a slave—a beloved brother. . . . If then you count me as a partner, receive him as you would me. But if he has wronged you or owes anything, put that on my account.

—PHILEMON V. 15–18

*K*ing Solomon once said, "There is a friend who sticks closer than a brother" (Proverbs 18:24). This truth is revealed in Paul's letter to Philemon, where we find him being that "friend who sticks closer than a brother" to Onesimus. Philemon was a wealthy entrepreneur in the city of Colossae. Paul had spent time there, winning Philemon to faith, and Philemon began a church in his own home. Onesimus was, in essence, under contract to Philemon and had stolen from him and split the scene. By the strangest of coincidences, Onesimus made his way to Rome to spend his take in the bright lights of the big city. There he was arrested and placed in a cell with Paul, who was imprisoned in Rome for preaching the gospel. Paul led him to Christ. Upon his release, Onesimus headed back in repentance to make restitution to Philemon. Paul wrote Philemon from his prison cell, assuring him of his love for and commitment to his new convert, and asking him to receive Onesimus back "no longer as a slave but . . . a beloved brother."

While Philemon and Onesimus share center stage in this relationship drama, the major behind-the-scenes part is played by Paul. He is the reconciler. He is the friend who sticks closer than a brother to both of these men. He stands between them—with Onesimus, the offending party, on one side and Philemon, the offended party, on the other side—and brings them together in reconciliation. And so, one with a truly repentant heart and the other with a truly receptive heart are brought back together as brothers.

Reconciliation only takes place when both parties do their part. The offending party must have a repentant heart, and the offended party must have a receptive heart that is empty of any resentment or desire for retaliation. Some relationships are never mended—not because the offending party is unrepentant, but because the offended party cannot seem to move beyond the need for revenge or retaliation. They simply cannot bring themselves to truly forgive, much less forget, and move on in reconciliation. But this *never* happens with Christ. The moment we come to Him in true repentance, He—like the prodigal son's father—receives us with the open arms of forgiveness. No clinched fists, no crossed arms, just open arms . . . wide, forgiving, loving, open arms.

There is a much deeper truth at play here in the book of Philemon than simply two people being reconciled to each other. In a very real sense, we are each Onesimus. *We* are the offending party. The Lord made us to have fellowship with Him, but we chose to go our own way and leave Him out of our lives. The Lord, like Philemon, is the offended party. God the Father provided a perfect paradise for all of us. But we thought we knew better and could do better, so we rebelled. Instead of washing His hands of us, God reached out in reconciliation by giving us the very best He had to offer: His own Son. But even that was not enough for us. We nailed His only Son to a cross of execution. Jesus invaded our space, our world. Why? In order to reconcile us to God the Father.

> Jesus invaded our space, our world. Why? In order to reconcile us to God the Father.

A part of our relationship with Jesus is found in our accountability to Him. Paul illustrated it in his letter to Philemon. In the final paragraph, Paul—not so subtly—said, "Oh, by the way, Philemon, prepare a guest room for me. I am coming your way" (Philemon v. 22, paraphrased). Can't you just picture Philemon now as he read Paul's letter, his chin cupped in his hands? The message surely came through loud and clear: *I am coming back to check up on you and to see how your relationship with Onesimus is going.* Only when we learn to be accountable to others, and to hold others accountable, will we understand what it means to be true brothers and sisters in Christ.

Jesus is here in Philemon . . . He is the true Friend who sticks closer than a brother, constantly reaching out to us in love to reconcile us to the Father.

50 FINDING JESUS IN HEBREWS

He Is the Final Word

God, who at various times and in various ways spoke in time past to the fathers by the prophets, has in these last days spoken to us by His Son, whom He has appointed heir of all things, through whom also He made the worlds.

—HEBREWS 1:1–2

It is always reassuring to hear the final word on something. Even as I type these words, I remember the anxiety as a kid of wondering if I made the football team—and the sweet relief of seeing my name on the list posted on the school's bulletin board. That list was the coach's final word. The same can be said for anyone who has tried out for a school play or musical. It is always good, after going through a long application process, to hear the final word and know we got a particular job. And I well remember after my own bout with cancer hearing my doctor's final word ten years ago, saying, "You are cancer free." Final words are memorable in the temporal matters of life and even more in the spiritual. We find Jesus here in the book of Hebrews. He is the final word on everything.

The writer of Hebrews declared that God spoke in the past "at various times and in various ways." Beginning with Adam, God spoke to us in "various times" throughout recorded Scripture:

- To Adam, God revealed Christ was coming to crush the serpent's head.
- To Abraham, God revealed Christ would come through a nation He would birth.
- To Jacob, God revealed Christ would come through the tribe of Judah.
- To Micah, God revealed that Christ would be born in Bethlehem.
- To Zechariah, God revealed Christ would be betrayed for thirty pieces of silver.
- To Isaiah, God revealed Christ would be wounded for our own transgressions.
- To David, God revealed that Christ would be crucified and pierced but would rise again.

God spoke not only "at various times" but "in various ways."

- At Mount Horeb, He spoke to Moses through a burning bush.
- At Mount Sinai, God spoke through thunder and lightning.

- To the prophet Elijah, God spoke through a still, small voice.
- To Ezekiel, God spoke in a vision.
- To Daniel, God spoke through dreams.
- To Balaam, God spoke through a donkey.
- To Jacob, God spoke through an angel.

Yes, God, at various times and in various ways, spoke to us in times past. But in this dispensation of grace in which we live, He has spoken to us "by His Son." Jesus is the final word. Period.

Jesus is the final word. Period.

The Old Testament is a book of shadows depicting progressive images of our coming Redeemer. The apostle Paul spoke of this as being "a shadow of things to come" (Colossians 2:17). There must be two elements in producing a shadow. To produce a shadow, there needs to be both a light and an image. Behind the words of Scripture, there is a great Light shining on the image of Christ and casting His shadow across its pages. As we observed in the introduction, the clarity of any shadow depends on the angle with which the light strikes the body. I can stand in the sunlight in the early morning hours when the sun is rising, and my shadow is completely out of proportion. It stretches all the way across the street and onto the building behind me. However, as the sun continues to rise, the shorter and more revealing my shadow becomes. At mid-morning, when the sun is at a forty-five-degree angle, my shadow is the perfect shape of my body. As I continue to stand in place and when the sun reaches its zenith at high noon, the shadow disappears and only my body is seen.

And so it is with the revelation of Christ in the Bible. When the Sun of revelation begins to shine way back in the early chapters of Genesis, the shadow is dim and a bit faint. As the chapters unfold and more light appears, Christ comes into sharper focus. By the time we reach Isaiah, chapter 53, there appears the perfect shadow of the One who would be "smitten by God, and afflicted . . . wounded for our transgressions, . . . bruised for our iniquities, . . . [and] led as a lamb to the slaughter" (vv. 4–5, 7). When we turn the page from Malachi 4:6 into the New Testament to Matthew 1:1, it is high noon on God's clock, the shadows disappear, and we see Jesus! No more shadows of Him. No more types. No more prophecies. Just Jesus, the final word of all things.

Of this final word, the apostle John said, "In the beginning was the Word, and the Word was with God, and the *Word was God.* . . . And the Word became flesh and dwelt among us, and we beheld His glory, the glory as of the only begotten of the Father, full of grace and truth" (John 1:1, 14, emphasis added). The incarnation is the most generous display of divine love to be found anywhere, at any time. God sent His final word to us, and His name is Jesus. What Jesus said to us in the Gospels needs no addendum or no addition. It is final. So much so that the apostle John closed Revelation, the last book of the Bible, with a word of warning—"If anyone adds to these things, God will add to him the plagues that are written in this book; and if anyone takes away from the words of the book of this prophecy, God shall take away his part from the Book of Life" (22:18–19). God is serious about His final word.

We find Jesus here in Hebrews. He is forever God's final word to you and me on any and every subject.

51 FINDING JESUS IN JAMES

He Is the Lord Who Heals the Sick

Is anyone among you sick? Let him call for the elders of the church, and let them pray over him, anointing him with oil in the name of the Lord. And the prayer of faith will save the sick, and the Lord will raise him up.

—JAMES 5:14–15

James, the half brother of Jesus and the leader of the Jerusalem church, wrote his letter to those new believers who had fled Jerusalem when they came under increasing persecution and were scattered across the Mediterranean world. His call was to be in touch with a hurting world. We live in the midst of such a world today.

Perhaps no other ministry of the New Testament church has seen as much perversion as the church's healing ministry. While many involved have pure hearts and worthy intentions, some healing ministries have too often been a vehicle for a few to build their own personal financial kingdoms by offering false hopes of healing to any and all who come their way. Here, in James 5, we find our Lord's only directive in all of Scripture concerning praying for those who are sick.

James began with a probing question, "Is anyone among

you sick?" The word we translate into the English *sick* means, in Greek, "without strength" or "to be weak." We often assume that physical sickness is all that is involved in healing. However, this word is directed to those who may be sick in spirit or soul as well as body. The recipients of James's letter had been forced to flee their homes and jobs. Tempted to give up, they had grown weary and weak.

James's proposal was for these people to call the elders of the church together so that they might "pray over [them], anointing [them] with oil in the name of the Lord." In the language of the New Testament, there are two distinct Greek words we translate into our English word *anoint*. One refers to an outward anointing, a "rubbing down with oil," which is found in the story of the good Samaritan who bandaged up a wounded stranger. The good Samaritan poured "oil and wine" on the man's wounds to fight infection and soothe the hurt (Luke 10:34). The other Greek word has to do with a ceremonial anointing used in a sacred and symbolic sense. This word is used when the Bible records that the Spirit "anointed" Jesus to preach the gospel (Luke 4:18). This type of anointing is closely akin to what happened in the parable on the Jericho Road. In other words, use the best medicine known to man. Support the efforts of those in the medical community to bring healing while still giving priority to the prayer of faith. James described a certain kind of prayer at the bed of one who is sick: he called it "the prayer of faith." Earlier in his letter, he indicated that when we pray, we must believe, asking "in faith, with no doubting, for he who doubts is like a wave of the sea driven and tossed by the wind" (James 1:6). The prayer of faith is always offered in accordance with two things: God's Word and God's will. Such a prayer must be grounded in God's Word, or it is not a prayer of faith. After all, in the words of Paul, "Faith comes by hearing, and hearing by the word of God" (Romans 10:17).

Finally, James made the provision plain: "The Lord will raise him up!" We find Jesus here in James. He is the Lord who heals the sick. Physical healing is a mystery wrapped up tight in the counsel of God's own will. Some say all can be healed. Yet Paul himself asked the Lord three times to remove his own "thorn in the flesh," only to discover that God gave him the grace to endure (2 Corinthians 12:7, 9).

> The prayer of faith is always offered in accordance with two things: God's Word and God's will.

All healing is divine. Medicine alone doesn't heal. Doctors alone do not heal. Proper diet alone doesn't heal. Exercise alone doesn't heal. Jesus heals! One of His own names in Scripture is *Jehovah-Rapha* . . . the God who heals. And we can trust the One who always has our best interests at heart.

Perhaps you know of someone who needs the Lord's healing hand. Remember, He is the Lord who never slumbers nor sleeps (Psalm 121:4). He is awake and aware. He is the same yesterday, today, and forever. Call some praying friends. Lean on them and their prayers, believe that our great God can still make the impossible possible, and surrender yourself into the loving hands of Jesus and His perfect will for your life. When you do, you will find Him . . . He is still the Lord who heals the sick.

52 FINDING JESUS IN FIRST AND SECOND PETER

He Is the Chief Shepherd

Shepherd the flock of God which is among you, serving as overseers, not by compulsion but willingly, not for dishonest gain but eagerly; nor as being lords over those entrusted to you, but being examples to the flock; and when the Chief Shepherd appears, you will receive the crown of glory that does not fade away.

—1 PETER 5:2–4

We have previously seen Jesus in the Psalms as the Shepherd. John, in his gospel, quoted Jesus who called Himself the "good shepherd" who "gives His life for the sheep" (John 10:11). The writer of Hebrews closed his letter by also referring to Jesus as the "great Shepherd" with these words: "Now may the God of peace who brought up our Lord Jesus from the dead, that great Shepherd of the sheep, through the blood of the everlasting covenant, make you complete in every good work to do His will, working in you what is well pleasing in His sight, through Jesus Christ, to whom be glory forever and ever. Amen" (13:20–21). Peter took it a notch higher by calling Jesus our "Chief Shepherd," who, upon His return, will present His faithful under-shepherds of His flock with "the crown of glory that does not fade away" (1 Peter 5:4).

Jesus is not just any shepherd; He is our good Shepherd. But He is not only good, He is great—our "great Shepherd." And, as if that were not descriptive enough, Peter identified Him as our "Chief Shepherd."

> Jesus is not just any shepherd; . . . Peter identified Him as our "Chief Shepherd."

Simon Peter was a shepherd to the first-century flock, the church of God. He became the undisputed leader of the Jerusalem church. When Paul burst forth from his post-conversion isolation of three years in Arabia and began to preach Christ, he first went to visit Peter in Jerusalem to make sure his teaching was in alignment with that of the apostolic tradition. In Paul's first letter, we read, "After three years I went up to Jerusalem to see Peter, and remained with him fifteen days" (Galatians 1:18). Peter was the greatest shepherd of the early church, and yet he referred to Jesus as "the Chief Shepherd." God has appointed a "Chief Shepherd" to oversee His own flock, and it is not me or you, nor was it Peter.

Jesus is the Chief Shepherd. Those called today as pastors of His local flocks are but under-shepherds—under His authority and command. As the Chief Shepherd, it is Jesus' responsibility to mend broken relationships. It is

His responsibility to save our country and appoint good and godly leaders when we deserve such. It is His ultimate responsibility to meet our needs. We, in ministry, are simply His representatives who are called to feed, lead, protect, and provide for His own sheep.

The faithful pastor has a special prize awaiting him. It is called the "pastor's crown." This reward is especially reserved for him and is spoken of by Peter in his first epistle: "Shepherd the flock of God . . . and when the Chief Shepherd appears, you will receive the crown of glory that does not fade away" (1 Peter 5:2–4). At His glorious appearing, when He comes again, Jesus will set the faithful pastor, His under-shepherd, apart from everyone else for an unusual recognition and reward. If you are a pastor reading these words, just think of it—the Chief Shepherd, the Lord Himself, will look you square in the eyes and say, "Well done, good and faithful servant" (Matthew 25:21). Then upon your head He will place the "crown of glory." All those times of being misunderstood and misrepresented, all those times of feeling unappreciated or unwelcome, will pale into nothingness at that moment on that glorious day. It will be worth it all.

At our wedding altar, as Susie and I knelt in prayer, a soloist softly sang the words of a hymn written by Dorothy Thrupp many years ago. It has been our constant prayer through the decades of our marriage. "Savior, like a shepherd lead us, much we need thy tender care; in Thy pleasant pastures feed us, for our use Thy folds prepare. . . . We are Thine, do Thou befriend us, be the guardian of our way; keep Thy flock, from sin defend us, seek us when we go astray. . . . Blessed Jesus, blessed Jesus, Thou hast loved us, love us still."

We find Jesus in the letters of Peter. He is not just our Shepherd, or our good Shepherd, or even our great Shepherd. He is, and ever will be, our Chief Shepherd.

53 FINDING JESUS IN FIRST, SECOND, AND THIRD JOHN

He Is Love

Again, a new commandment I write to you, which thing is true in Him and in you, because the darkness is passing away, and the true light is already shining. He who says he is in the light, and hates his brother, is in darkness until now. He who loves his brother abides in the light, and there is no cause for stumbling in him.

—1 JOHN 2:8–10

*T*he apostle John was the apostle of love. Six times in his gospel, when referencing himself, he identified himself as "the apostle whom Jesus loved." Like a thread woven through the fabric of his three brief letters, containing only seven short chapters, is the word *love*, appearing thirty-four different times. John provided us with the best definition of our Lord, and he used only three words, "God is love" (1 John 4:8). His letters are filled with nuggets pertaining to the love of Christ: "Behold what manner of love the Father has bestowed on us, that we should be called children of God!" (3:1); "In this is love, not that we loved God, but that He loved us and sent His Son to be the propitiation for our sins" (4:10); "There is no fear in love; but perfect love casts out fear" (v. 18); and the needed reminder that "we love Him because He first loved us" (v. 19).

In 1 John 2:8, John spoke of "a new commandment." He was referring back to the words of his gospel, when he quoted our Lord on the eve of the crucifixion, "A new commandment I give to you, that you love one another; as I have loved you, that you also love one another" (John 13:34). This "new commandment" was to supersede all the others not only in attitude but in action. This is not a mere suggestion or an option for the believer. It is a commandment with all the authority of the Father, Son, and Holy Spirit behind it.

Before Jesus gave us that new commandment, the very best we could do was to live on the level of the old commandment. This old commandment is found in Leviticus 19:18 and was referenced earlier in the Gospels when Jesus spoke of the Great Commandment (Matthew 22:36–40). The old commandment called on us to "love your neighbor as yourself." But it was a love with limits, conditioned by such things as time or conduct, situations or social standing, even self-respect. It can be changeable and fickle at times.

True love is now expressed in the "new commandment." For thirty-three years, Jesus gave us a picture of how such love is to be evidenced. In essence, Jesus said, "For three decades now I have shown you real love. I am about to leave you, but before I go, a new commandment I am giving you. No longer are you to love one another as you love yourself, but from this moment on you are to love each other *as I have loved you*."

This new commandment calls on us to love as Jesus loved: unconditionally. On our own, we are completely incapable of loving on that level. The only way this kind of love becomes possible for us is through experientially knowing the love of Christ in our own hearts by faith. Once we receive His love into our hearts unconditionally, we are then able to release it to others in the same way.

In order to love as Jesus did, we are to love one another not only unconditionally but also with a love that is unlimited. Because Jesus' love for us has no limits. Nothing "shall be able to separate us from the love of God which is in Christ Jesus our Lord" (Romans 8:39). This higher-level love is utterly unselfish, so much so that it took Jesus all the way to the cross. And we should also note that it is unchangeable. As the writer of Hebrews said, "Jesus Christ is the same yesterday, today, and forever" (13:8). Under this new commandment, we are not to love others merely as we love ourselves; rather, we are to love others as Jesus has loved us—unconditionally, without limits, unselfishly, and unchanging.

> This new commandment calls on us to love as Jesus loved: unconditionally.

And what did John say is the result of our living our lives on this higher level of love? He said this is the mark by which everyone will know that we are Christ's followers: "if you have love for one another" (John 13:35). Perhaps John put it best in his first letter when he said, "Beloved, let us love one another, for love is of God; and everyone who loves is born of God and knows God. He who does not love does not know God, for God is love" (1 John 4:7–8). And in the same letter he wrote, "We know that we have passed from death to life, because we love the brethren" (3:14).

Love is the oxygen of the kingdom. Let Jesus love you. Then love others with His unconditional love, because there "now abide faith, hope, love, these three; but the greatest of these is love" (1 Corinthians 13:13). We find Jesus here in the letters of John, the apostle "whom Jesus loved." And he framed it best when he simply defined our Lord in one word—*love*!

54   FINDING JESUS IN JUDE

He Is the One Who Keeps Us from Falling

Now to Him who is able to keep you from stumbling, and to present you faultless before the presence of His glory with exceeding joy, to God our Savior, who alone is wise, be glory and majesty, dominion and power, both now and forever. Amen.

—JUDE vv. 24–25

*F*or most of his brief letter, Jude spoke in the third person as he addressed the dark days of apostasy coming to the church. But as he concluded his epistle, he moved to the second person, as if to get up close and personal with us in his closing thoughts. He ended his message on a note of hope with words intended to assure us that we can make it. Jude pointed us to Jesus, who "is able to keep you from stumbling, and to present you faultless" before His Father's throne. We find Jesus here in Jude—as the One who keeps us from falling.

Jude began his letter by reminding readers that Jesus "*is* able" (emphasis added). Our Lord's heroics are not confined to the bygone days we read about in Scripture. Jude did not say that Jesus *was* able. Nor are we simply dealing with a God who is powerless in the present but offers bright hope for tomorrow if we can just hold on. Jude also did not say that He *will be* able. Instead, he wrote, "To Him who *is* able." Right now. God was able in the past, and He will be able in the future. But the good news is that Jesus *is* also able to meet our every need, right now in the present.

Jude bookended his letter with strong words about our eternal security in Christ. In the opening verse, he affirmed the eternal security of the believer when he said that we are not only called and sanctified by God the Father but "preserved in Jesus Christ" (Jude v. 1). And on the back end, he framed it thus: "To Him who is able to keep you from stumbling." Jude wanted us to know that in Jesus we are secure in the now life as well as in the next life.

We live in an uncertain world today. Think about it. It is uncertain politically, economically, materially, socially, nationally, internationally, and in just about any other dimension imaginable. But in the midst of all this uncertainty, God wants us to know we can be secure in this life. He is able to keep us from falling. Jude chose his words carefully here. He insisted that Jesus is able to keep us from "stumbling." Stumbling is usually the act that precedes a fall. God is not simply able to keep us from falling, but even better, He is able to keep us from stumbling.

In the midst of all this uncertainty, God wants us to know we can be secure in this life.

Jude continued his reassurances by explaining that we are not simply secure in the now life but in the next life as well. Jesus will one day "present you faultless before the presence of His glory with exceeding joy" (Jude v. 24). Not a single one of us is "faultless" today. We all have our secret sins and shortcomings. But in that day that is to come, Jesus Himself will present us faultless before the Father's throne. The Bible says, "Beloved, now we are children of God; and it has not yet been revealed what we shall be, but we know that when He is revealed, we shall be like Him, for we shall see Him as He is" (1 John 3:2). This is an awesome thought: "We shall be like Him." Because He is without blemish or spot. How can this be? When we are saved, we are immediately justified in the Father's eyes by Christ. Jesus' blood cleanses us from all sin. As we grow in Christ's grace and knowledge, we are progressively sanctified by His grace. And, on that grand and glorious day of which Jude wrote, we shall be presented faultless before the throne.

That presentation before the throne will be made "with exceeding joy." It was the anticipation of this joy that helped our Lord endure the cross. This is the truth at the heart of the Hebrews writer's statement when he called on us to look to "Jesus, the author and finisher of our faith, who for the joy that was set before Him endured the cross, despising the shame, and has sat down at the right hand of the throne of

God" (12:2). This "joy that was set before Him" is the joy He finds in presenting us faultless before His Father's throne. When Jude laid down his pen, all that was left to say was "Amen."

We find Jesus here in Jude. He is the One who keeps us from falling. And so we join Jude's own "amen" as he wrote, "To God our Savior who alone is wise, be glory and majesty, dominion and power, both now and forever. Amen" (Jude v. 25). Amen and amen.

55

FINDING JESUS IN REVELATION

He Is the Alpha and the Omega

"I am the Alpha and the Omega, the Beginning and the End, the First and the Last."

—REVELATION 22:13

*A*lpha is the first letter and Omega is the last letter of the Greek alphabet. When Jesus declared Himself to be the "Alpha and Omega," He was saying that He was the beginning and the ending of all things. He always existed, and He always will exist. "All things were made through Him, and without Him nothing was made that was made" (John 1:3). Jesus is the first and last of everything. He is the "author and finisher" of our faith (Hebrews 12:2). Jesus is in the first verse of Genesis, and He is in the last verse of Revelation. And, as we have seen in the preceding chapters, we find Him in every book of the Bible in between. Yes, He is "the Alpha and Omega, the Beginning and the End, the First and the Last" . . . of everything!

Not only is Jesus prominent in Genesis 1:1, but He also has the last word in Revelation 22:20. The final spoken words of men and women are always intriguing. Here on the last page of the Bible, we have the last promise of the Bible coming straight from the final recorded words of our Lord, "Surely I am coming quickly." And each generation since the moment these words escaped His lips has been "looking for the blessed hope and [His] glorious appearing" (Titus 2:13). There are thousands of promises in the Bible. But this final one recorded in Revelation 22:20—though yet to be fulfilled—marks the climax of all of human history.

The Bible speaks of three major comings. First the coming of Christ, born of a virgin in the small, obscure little village of Bethlehem. He came and "dwelt among us" (John 1:14). For thirty-three years Jesus showed us a picture of true love incarnated into human flesh. However, most did not recognize Him. At best, most thought He was just another "one of the prophets" (Matthew 16:14).

The second major coming foretold in the Bible is the coming of the Holy Spirit, as was prophesied in Joel. This coming took place on the day of Pentecost when the Holy Spirit came to indwell the believers, never to leave us, empowering us for His service. In the old dispensation, the Holy Spirit came upon people, but when they became unfaithful, He left them. One of the saddest verses of Scripture is when the Bible records that the Holy Spirit "had departed" from Samson (Judges 16:20). King David, in his prayer of repentance, pleaded with the Father, "Do not take Your Holy Spirit from me" (Psalm 51:11). But today, in the dispensation of grace, no believer need ever pray that prayer. When we come to know Christ, the Holy Spirit comes to reside in us and promises that He will never leave us.

The only major coming yet to be fulfilled is the promised return, the second coming of Christ. For just as He came the first time, He will come again: "Surely I am coming quickly."

On the last page of the Bible, we not only see the last recorded promise but also the last recorded prayer of the Bible. Having heard this amazing promise from His Savior's lips, John burst out in prayer, "Even so, come, Lord Jesus! (Revelation 22:20). Just five words, but so powerful in their intensity. In his prayer, John anticipated this great event, the return of our Lord Jesus to usher in a millennium of peace on the earth, followed by the splendor of eternal endless ages with Him in heaven where "God will wipe away every tear from their eyes; there shall be no more death, nor sorrow, nor crying. There shall be no more pain, for the former things have passed away" (Revelation 21:4). Following this incredible promise, Jesus said to John, "It is done! I am the Alpha and the Omega, the Beginning and the End. I will give of the fountain of the water of life freely to him who thirsts"

(v. 6). No wonder John's first impulse was to pray, "Even so"—just as You have promised, Lord, come—"Come, Lord Jesus!"

We come now to the close of *The Bible Code* with the reminder that the Lord Jesus is the First and the Last of all things. He is the Author and the Finisher of our faith. He is the Beginning and the End of everything. He is *everything*. We find Him here in Revelation . . . He is the Alpha and the Omega. And in closing, whoever we are and wherever we are, we join John in praying, "Even so, come, Lord Jesus! The grace of our Lord Jesus Christ be with you all. Amen" (Revelation 22:20–21).

EPILOGUE

*A*s we have journeyed through the Bible, we have found Jesus in every book. He is there from Genesis 1:1 to Revelation 22:21. The Bible is the Jesus Book. During His sojourn here on earth, Jesus challenged His followers—and us—to "search the Scriptures, for in them you think you have eternal life; and these are they which testify of Me" (John 5:39). And so we have in *The Bible Code*, and we have found that the Scriptures do, indeed, testify of Him.

There is a scarlet thread of redemption that runs through every book of the Bible until it culminates on a hill outside the city walls of Jerusalem. There, Jesus took our sin so that we could take His righteousness. There, Jesus died our death so that we could live His life.

It may be that, while you were journeying through those pages, God's Spirit has been nudging you to put your faith and trust in Christ for the forgiveness of your sin in order to receive the gift of eternal life. Heaven is God's personal and free gift to you. It cannot be earned, nor will you ever deserve it. We are all sinners who have fallen short of God's perfect standard for our lives. Yes, God is a God of love, but He is also a God of justice and therefore must punish sin. This is where Jesus steps in. He is the holy and sinless God-man who came to take your sins upon His own body and to die on the cross as punishment for those sins. Just knowing this fact is not enough, though. You must transfer your trust from yourself and your own human efforts to Christ alone, placing your faith in Him and in Him alone.

Jesus said, "Behold, I stand at the door and knock. If anyone hears My voice and opens the door, I will come in to him" (Revelation 3:20). If you would like to receive this free gift of eternal life, call on Jesus right now, at this very moment. He promised, "Whoever calls on the name of the Lord shall be saved" (Romans 10:13). The following is a suggested prayer you can pray from your own heart.

Dear Lord Jesus,
I know I have sinned. I know that, in and of myself,
I don't deserve eternal life. Please forgive me for my
sin. Thank You for taking my sin upon Your own body
and dying on the cross on my behalf. I trust in You as
the only One who can save me from eternal separa-
tion from a holy God. Come into my life right now.
I accept Your free and gracious offer of forgiveness,
abundant life, and eternal life. Thank You, Lord, for
coming into life as my Savior and Lord.

A simple prayer cannot save you. But Jesus can and will.

If this prayer expresses the desire of your heart, you can claim the promise Jesus made to those who believe in Him: "Most assuredly . . . he who believes in Me has everlasting life" (John 6:47).

You can now join millions of Christ's followers in answering Pilate's question, "What then shall I do with Jesus who is called Christ?" (Matthew 27:22) by confidently affirming, "I believe Jesus is the one and only Savior, and I place my trust in Him now and for eternity."

MISSION:DIGNITY

$\mathscr{A}$ll the author's royalties and any additional proceeds from the Code series (including *The Bible Code*) go to the support of Mission:Dignity, a ministry that enables thousands of retired ministers (and, in most cases, their widows) who are living near the poverty level to live out their days with dignity and security. Many of them spent their ministries in small churches that were unable to provide adequately for their retirement. They also lived in church-owned parsonages and had to vacate them upon their vocational retirement as well. Mission:Dignity tangibly shows these good and godly servants they are not forgotten and will be cared for in their declining years.

All the expenses for this ministry are paid out of an endowment that has already been raised. Consequently, anyone who gives to Mission:Dignity can be assured that every cent of their gift goes straight to one of these precious saints in need.

Find out more by visiting www.missiondignity.org and click on the Mission:Dignity icon or call toll-free 877-888-9409.

ABOUT THE AUTHOR

For more than twenty years, O. S. Hawkins served pastorates at the First Baptist Church in Fort Lauderdale, Florida, and in Dallas, Texas. A native of Fort Worth, he has earned four degrees (BBA, MDiv, DMin, and PhD). He is president of GuideStone Financial Resources, the world's largest Christian screened mutual fund with over $17 billion in assets serving over 50,000 churches. He is the bestselling author of the Code series, including *The Joshua Code* and *The Jesus Code*, which has sold over 1.5 million copies. He speaks regularly at conferences and churches across the nation.

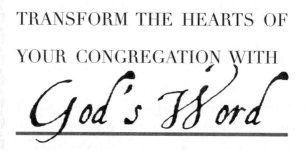

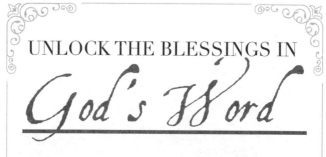